Rhythm of the Sea

Rhythm of the Sea

Ramya Chamalie Jirasinghe

First published 2007

Published by
Hambantota District Chamber of Commerce (HDCC)
Tangalle Road, Hambantota, Sri Lanka
chamber@hdcc.lk
www.hdcc.lk

ISBN 978-955-50218-0-7

Principal photography Denise Militzer
Additional photography and illustrations: HDCC, Samir Shah, Chatura Kodikara
Photos © - individual photographers

Designed and typeset by Deshan Tennekoon
Printed and bound in Sri Lanka by Gunaratne Offset Ltd

FRONTISPIECE: The Hambantota beach: a wave has been captured in the moment of "sudden complete silence" that Woolf describes.

For the people of
Hambantota

THIS BOOK HAS BEEN SPONSORED and supported by the **Hambantota District Chamber of Commerce (HDCC)**. The vision of HDCC's founders is to act as the 'gateway' for development, ensuring social cohesion and economic success of the Hambantota District.

It is a vision that has given the organisation the ability to continuously develop and pioneer projects that would transform the Hambantota District to give its people a quality of life and advantage similar to that of the more privileged districts of Sri Lanka. To find out more about the HDCC, to support it projects or assist the people and places cited in this book, please visit **www.hdcc.lk**

The HDCC is deeply indebted to:
- Ruvanthi Sivapragasam, for managing the project with efficiency and immense patience
- Voluntary Service Overseas, Sri Lanka, for a sustained partnership of over a decade
- Samson Abeykoon, President and the Board of Directors of the HDCC for taking ownership of the project
- Mr. M. A. Piyasena, District Secretary, Hambantota for his encouragement and for providing us with a wealth of information
- Keerthi Munasingha, President, Hambantota Traders Association
- Ranjith Muthumala, Vice President, HDCC
- WUSC Uniterra volunteer David Book, who made the HDCC Tsunami Report, which was the foundation for this book, a reality
- The HDCC staff who contributed, especially S.R.G Dammika, Krishanthi Weerasinghe and Rizmi Zakariya
- WUSC Uniterra volunteer Denise Militzer of Ruhunu Rural Womens Organisation
- M. R. Hassim of Hambantota for field coordination
- All those individuals who willingly shared their thoughts and experiences and permitted us to publish their stories in this book.

Acknowledgments

THIS BOOK BEGAN in the hearts of two people: Azmi Thassim and Ruvanthi Sivapragasam. I am deeply grateful to them for trusting me with a project which was one of their personal dreams. Their humour, wry comments and the tight reign they kept on their natural leanings towards "management", gave me all the support and freedom needed to write this book.

Tissa Jayatilaka, Executive Director, United States—Sri Lanka Fulbright Commission, Dr. SinhaRaja Tammita-Delgoda, Prof. Katherine Hoffman and Andy Mason helped revise the manuscript and provided invaluable suggestions and comments.

The mind—reading book designer Deshan Tennekoon, Shehan de Silva, Denise Militzer, Rashmee Thiyagalingam, the staff of HDCC, my colleagues at the Fulbright Commission, Soraya Usuf, Nithashi Thassim, Krishanthi Weerasinghe, Samir Shah, Nadeeka Senadhira, B.L. Ramanayake, Ranjith Muthumala and Keerthi Munasinghe contributed to this book in numerous irreplaceable ways.

My family, especially my parents, gave me their loving support and the time away from all domestic duties without a word of complaint.

Sanjeev Hewavitharne proved a true friend, making unasked for comments, providing excellent dinner company in Hambantota and brewing perfect cups of coffee.

Not surprisingly, it was my three year-old daughter who put things into perspective by giving me a sense of the distances from Colombo to the end of the universe and to Hambantota.

Contents

....

*Profiles of people from Hambantota as they recount
the tsunami and discuss their lives today:*

Kalutara beach
January 1, 2004

Image by DigitalGlobe

Kalutara beach
December 26, 2004

Image by DigitalGlobe

The Wave

All the year round day and night, if you looked down that long two-mile line of sea and sand, you would see, unless it was very rough, continually at regular intervals a wave, not very high but unbroken two miles long, lift itself up very slowly, wearily, poise itself for a moment in sudden complete silence, and then fall with a great thud upon the sand. That moment of complete silence followed by the great thud, the thunder of the wave upon the shore, became part of the rhythm of my life.

.... the rhythm of the sea, the rhythm of Hambantota.[1]

Leonard Woolf, *Growing* (1967)

A damaged house in Hambantota Town.

MOST OF THE PEOPLE who did see a wave rise from the sea around Sri Lanka on the 26th of December 2004 never survived it. The few who lived to speak about the moment when the sea lifted itself into a towering wave, a vertical sheet of water hunched and foaming at the edge that covered the horizon before it fell thundering onto the land, remember being engulfed by a terrible darkness. For others, the wave came in as a sound. A blast so powerful, so deafening and yet hollow that they thought everything around them had been shattered by the wind. Many have no memory of what happened immediately before the wave. They remember only the horror of the water suddenly engulfing them and of being swept by its force towards loss and survival. In a hundred different ways, now recollected as personal memories, the tsunami crashed into Sri Lanka on a quiet Sunday morning.[2]

The word tsunami is the Japanese word for 'harbour wave'[3]. According to the U.S. National Weather Service,

> Tsunamis, also called seismic sea waves or, incorrectly, tidal waves, generally are caused by earthquakes, less commonly by submarine landslides, infrequently by submarine volcanic eruptions and very rarely by a large meteorite impact in the ocean. Submarine volcanic eruptions have the potential to produce truly awesome tsunami waves.[4]

The tsunami of the 26th of December was caused by an earthquake of 9.3 magnitude that took place in the North Western coast off the Indonesian island of Sumatra. The earthquake was the second largest since the invention of the seismometer 100 years ago[5] and was the largest earthquake in 40 years. It caused a complex slip on the 'fault' where the oceanic portion of the Indian Plate slides under Sumatra, a part of the Eurasian Plate, and deformed the ocean floor, pushing the overlying water up into a tsunami wave.

The first wave arrived in Sumatra on the 26th morning at 6.58, local time. In about 2 hours the waves had reached Sri Lanka, when it was just past 9.00 am in the Eastern and South Eastern coasts of the island. On the West coast, according to residents, clocks that stopped because of seawater recorded 9.20 am. The point above sea level of a tsunami when it rises from the sea, known as the run-up elevation, ranged from less than 3 meters to over 12 meters around the Sri Lankan coast. The water level was highest along the Eastern and Southern coasts.[6] The impact of the wave and the elevation of the wave differed depending on the topography. Where the sea was shallowest, the run-up elevation was highest. Mangroves and sand-dunes saved a few areas from devastation. Early warning mechanisms for earthquakes in the region were weak and failed to save lives.

Only animals escaped, not by chance, but by some instinctive sense that had been wired into their biological and sensorial systems which compelled them away from the disaster. According to the *US Geological Survey*; "Both domestic and wild animals were seen evacuating to higher ground long before the tsunami arrived on the south coast of Sri Lanka."[7] Close to the *Ruhuna National Park (Yala)* in Hambantota[8], many people lost their lives. However, the gamekeepers did not find many animal carcasses.

More than 230,000 people from around the world died or were reported missing from the tsunami. 1.2 million people were displaced. In December 2005, Sri Lanka confirmed 30,322 deaths and disappearances from the tsunami. Over 516,150 people were displaced and the estimated overall damage to Sri Lanka was US$ 1 billion.[9]

For the people who were caught in the tsunami and were devastated by the losses it wrought, the 26th of December 2004 will be the darkest moment in their lives. The sea transformed into a monster: murderous and unpredictable. Over time, however, the coastal communities' fear of going back to the very places that were devastated and razed to the ground has lessened. The entire coastline that was affected by the tsunami in Sri Lanka, which two years ago was a shamble of debris, is now beginning to return to what it looked like before December 2004. Today, most people have gone back to the sea and the beach. They have returned to it for their livelihood, for their evening swim and for their family outing. Houses have come up where hundreds of lives were lost. But the signs of the tsunami are there. The look of normalcy that greets the visitor now is not the normalcy of the past but that of the present where changes wrought by the devastation have been embedded into places and lives. Like 'before', children are going back to school. Yet, unlike before, many of these children do not live where they once did and some no longer have their own families. The faintest rumour of an earthquake in the ocean sends the coastal communities into disarray: people start running, families grab their belongings and leave their homes, everybody rushes to get away and the day turns into a nightmare.

While the survivors are teetering on the brink of moving on from the events of the tsunami, many of them are still struggling to define their new lives. They are trying to understand the future that has been offered to them. For survivors this new unknown future has taken the form of a house they never owned or the prospect of better living conditions, but their new life will always be one that was catalysed by a tremendous loss. In some parts of coastal Sri Lanka, entire communities and regions are re-creating themselves this way. Hambantota is one such area. The tsunami created overwhelming loss and chaos in the District, but even there, people's lives have regained the "rhythm of the sea".

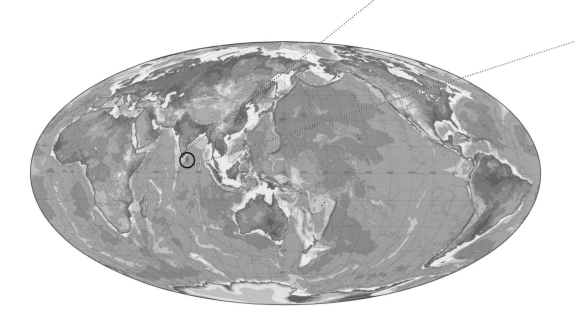

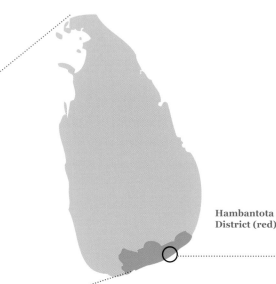

**Hambantota
District (red)**

A rough sketch of an initial area-assessment prepared for the Urban Development Authority by a volunteer planning team of architects; Varuna de Silva, Pradeep Kodikara, Sanath Liyanage, Arosha Perera, and US Fulbright Scholar Samir Shah; after the team's first visit to Kirinda, in Hambantota, on January 8, 2005.

The drawing overlays the extent of damage over the original town, and was used by the planners for orientation to the scale of the disaster.

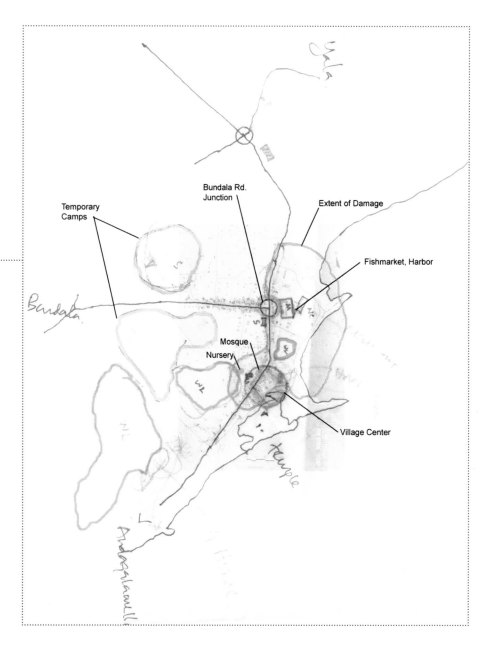

Temporary
Camps

Bundala Rd.
Junction

Extent of Damage

Fishmarket, Harbor

Mosque

Nursery

Village Center

Hambantota

But, in reality, one never sees Hambantota – one feels it. Maybe, you yourself have sensed this when lolling one late evening on the verandah of the Rest House under a sky of blazing stars; or when a moon, dark yellow, was rising in the east. Some have traced this mystery to its harsh night-smells of cooling earth mingling with the tang of the sea. Yet others to its day-time odours of sweat, dried fish, and dust.[10]

R.L. Brohier, *Seeing Ceylon* (1971)

Trishaws, motorcycles, cars, buses and pedestrians compete for space on the narrow A2 highway.

THE RAILWAY never reaches Hambantota. It makes its way as far as Matara and stops, forcing travellers destined for Hambantota who use the train to continue the remainder of the journey, another two hours, by road.

There are two frequently used highways to Hambantota from the rest of the country. They capture the essence of Hambantota: the sea and the dry zone. The A2 highway goes through Hambantota tracing the outer edges of the country as it makes its way from Colombo to Wellawaya. The road follows the South-western coast of the island and then winds up towards the plains from the deep-south. It takes the traveller as close as it can to the ocean. In certain places along the way, the road almost touches the rocks that line the beach preventing the sea from eroding the land. The sound of the sea and the faint smell of saltwater fill the air. The best time to travel along this road is in the evening when the sun is about to set. On a bright day, at some point of the traveller's journey, the sky will change from clear blue-white to candy floss pinks and oranges. The sun will hang tantalizingly above the horizon – a massive orange pomelo, contemplating the day. Then it will suddenly plunge into the ocean and fall off the edge of the world.

In Sinhala, Tamil and English, the road sign confirms that the traveller has arrived in Hambantota.

The other route to Hambantota is the path of the A18 highway. Unlike the A2, this road makes Hambantota its purpose. It branches off from another highway. The road begins in the mountain ranges that surround the central highlands of the country. The journey is therefore one of inescapable contrasts. The start is lush and green. The trees are heavy with foliage and the atmosphere is always humid. This doesn't last. Soon, the road begins to make its way through the wide plain that is shared by the Ratnapura, Monaragala and the Hambantota Districts. Everything in this area is dry and brittle. The trees are scraggy: the ground is covered with a harsh scrub. There is the unmistakable sense that nature is no longer hospitable here. It will not suffer the fragile or the fainthearted; only the weatherworn and the tenacious will make it. The dry zone takes up about a third of Hambantota and most of it is jungle that has been carved into nature reserve: the home of elephants, leopards and bears. Yala, one of the oldest nature reserves in Sri Lanka, forms part of Hambantota in the East. Scattered around are several other wildlife conservation parks including bird sanctuaries.

Geography has always played a vital role in the area's identity. In the days of the ancient kingdoms, as far back as 200 BC, the deep-south, which included the area now known as Hambantota, formed the *Kingdom of Ruhuna*. The kingdom was coveted for its agricultural produce that was sustained by a network of reservoirs: rice was the staple crop. The region also offered contact with the outside world through its coastal setting. The Southern coastline of Sri Lanka has several natural harbours. These harbours lay on one of the *Silk Routes* taken by traders criss-crossing between the Far East and the West. The Far Easterners who used the *Silk Route*, travelled in the *sampan*: a flat bottomed wooden boat that is still used in Malaysia, Indonesia and Vietnam.[11] It is believed that *Hamban* is a corruption of the word *sampan*. *"Tota"* is the Sinhala word for *harbour. Hambantota* was therefore the *"sampan-harbour"*. [12]

Hambantota Town is multi ethnic. However, while a few small villages that are scattered along the coast are inhabited by Muslim people, the rest of Hambantota is predominantly

Sinhalese. The different communities, the Sinhala, the Tamil, the Malay, and the Moor were by necessity interdependent for their survival, particularly commercial. While this engendered tolerance between them, each community maintained its own boundary and identity. Very briefly, the tsunami threw this society into disarray. The delicate lines of individual and communal definition that had kept communities apart were broken.

Hambantota was one of the most severely damaged regions of the country by the tsunami in 2004. It tolled the second largest loss of lives[13] in Sri Lanka. The physical devastation was incalculable and the turmoil it brought upon people who had survived within fragile human-made boundaries in a difficult geographic setting was indescribable. Suddenly, the coastal communities' way of life was shattered. Their world was turned into chaos.

Over the last two years, Hambantota and its people have forced themselves to rise from the upheaval. This is a new journey on a road to a Hambantota that is different to what it was before the tsunami. Yet, this journey is constantly affected, vicariously driven by each decision made at the 'centre' in Colombo and therefore individual lives and the fate of a distant region are inevitably at the mercy of the direction taken by the larger forces of politics and governance of the nation. No one knows where the journey will end.

National
Relief Operations

THE PRESIDENT of Sri Lanka was out of the country when the tsunami disaster occurred. For a brief time, less than 48 hours, the Prime Minister, who became the President the following year, took over national relief work. When the President returned, she set up the *Centre for National Operations* (CNO) with Dr. Tara De Mel who was at the time the Secretary to the Ministry of Higher Education and a trusted friend, as its head. The CNO was housed in the Presidential Secretariat, a neo-classical building which was constructed by the British as the home of the first parliament of Sri Lanka. As the Presidential Secretariat, the building has been under high security for many years. Anyone entering is subject to rigorous, time consuming security checks which were not relaxed even at the time it housed the CNO. Yet, the President brought all the relevant line ministries, the armed forces, the international aid & relief organisations and the non-governmental organisations to a centralised place within this building: the CNO worked from one large wood-panelled room, lit with dripping chandeliers.

From the CNO, the central government of Sri Lanka tried to take stock of the unfolding humanitarian crisis as numbers of the people dead and displaced filtered in from the coastal districts. At the same time, the government had to manage the disaster, provide relief and coordinate the influx of humanitarian aid that came in from overseas. Sri Lanka did not have a comprehensive disaster management plan to deal with a crisis of the magnitude of the tsunami. The country also lacked professionals with disaster

Tents were the first form of shelter provided to the displaced people in the immediate aftermath of the tsunami.

Over time, temporary shelters became semi-permanent structures as displaced people attempted to create a home out of their new surroundings.

management expertise and had no procedures or processes to be put into action in the event of a large-scale disaster. The CNO therefore had to contend not only with the relief work, but also with the task of creating logistics and procedures for its own functioning. Communication systems and processes had to be established; computers had to be brought in and networked; information had to be gathered, collated and shared within the Centre. Chaos was inevitable.

David Evans, today the Chief Technical Advisor to UN-Habitat, was in charge of co-ordinating the Non Governmental Organisations at the CNO. He describes how everyone worked round the clock within the Centre and how effective the military was at getting relief to the people and at managing the evacuation work in devastated areas. While local and foreign institutions and systems within the country were attempting to deal with the crisis, the CNO had to simultaneously manage the hundreds of organisations and people who poured in from around the world offering aid and their time. Individuals, aid organisations, military from other nations and teams of professionals who had a few days or weeks to spare had come to Sri Lanka at their own expense and offered their services. All of them would eventually turn up at the CNO for advice on where their assistance was needed. It is fascinating to listen to David Evans for as he talks, he is also looking back on the 6 weeks where so much was achieved by the CNO despite chaos, mismanagement, internal politics and individual differences.

We discuss that in retrospect, a unit such as the CNO can be measured for effectiveness by what it averted: the prevention of an immediate humanitarian health crisis by containing communicable diseases, hunger and lack of shelter. Within 48 hours most of the people were receiving State sponsored aid and almost all had been evacuated to temporary shelter.

However, in retrospect, the offers of aid, volunteers' time, equipment received and information collected could have been used more effectively. Volunteers could have been hassled less if they had been initially met at the airport instead of being sent from pillar to post until they found their way to the CNO. The information within the CNO could have been shared more effectively among its own staff to begin with, thereby avoiding embarrassingly contradictory statements that came out from the CNO. The CNO could have been housed in a building with easier access to the public and to the staff. Finally, the CNO's systems, procedures and data should have been handed over to the organisation that was to be set up for carrying on the rehabilitation work following on from the relief work. This is all clear in retrospect. None of these ideal scenarios took place during the life-time of the CNO. And, systems have not been set in place for these procedures to come into effect in the event of another such crisis in the country.

In the long term, the country also failed to take advantage of the opportunity to catalyse momentous development oriented changes. The 2.1 billion U.S. dollars of aid that was pledged to the government was sufficient for long term reconstruction projects, which in conjunction with national and regional level planning, would have had a significant impact on the development goals of the country. The opening for all these possibilities closed within the first year as the country fractured once again along the familiar lines of political and ethnic differences.

Yet, the first basis of evaluation of an organisation such as the CNO should always be the degree to which it averted an immediate humanitarian disaster in the first 72 hours. On this, the CNO, riding on the complementary effects of a culture of community service among the people, proved to be remarkably effective. It was a baseline that the U.S.A, equipped with better systems and resources, ranked low on in the wake of a series of natural disasters a year later.

The CNO was closed down unexpectedly six weeks after the tsunami following allegations of possible misuse of power and funds by key officials. The room at the Presidential Secretariat was cleared, the equipment disconnected and the files and data sealed in boxes. The staff were asked to leave immediately. Today, the hall is once again a large, empty, wood panelled room.

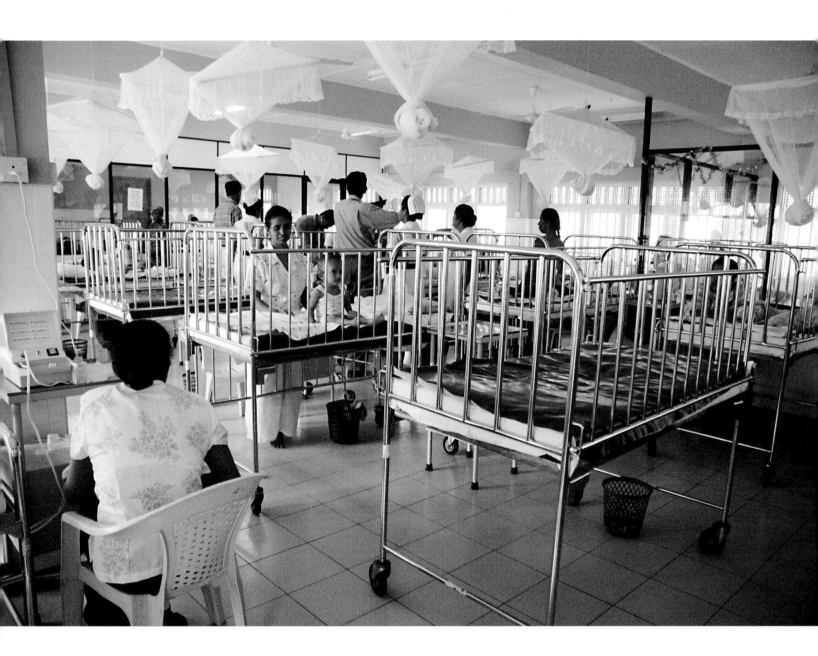

Gifts

IT IS TEN DAYS after the tsunami. Nick Buckingham and Franz Meyer sit in Nick's house in Tangalle and wonder "what they could do to help." [14] Nick is from Britain and Franz from New Zealand. Both of them have been in Tangalle for over 5 years. Their meeting each other in Tangalle, three years ago, was inevitable in this small community where everybody knows each other. Franz has taken on the Financial Administrator's role for the boutique hotel project that Nick is developing. Yet now, in the wake of the tsunami, there are rumours that the government will impose a 100 meter building reservation from the beach, preventing new constructions within this zone. This puts Nick's hotel project on hold.

As they chat, Nick mentions that his company in Britain has promised to raise fifty thousand pounds for him to use on tsunami relief work in Sri Lanka. The two men throw around ideas of what to do with the money. They could build a few houses. Yet in a small community, especially in one in which most of the displaced are known to them, it would mean having to select a few recipients and leave others out. Franz was at home in Tangalle on the day of the tsunami and treated a severely injured British tourist who lost her child. Having experienced the need for better medical facilities to deal with such a crisis, he suggests a community medical centre. This idea grows. Nick says they should use the money on the Tangalle District Hospital: an underutilised hospital, badly serviced and in disrepair. The Tangalle Hospital Project is born.

The funds for the Isabella Children's Ward in the Tangalle Hospital were raised for the Buckingham Tsunami Relief Project by a British family in memory of their daughter, Isabella, who died in the tsunami when they were holidaying in Tangalle.

The response of the public through donations, both locally and globally, to the tsunami crisis was enormous and has never been seen before or since. While this speaks of the altruism that people are capable of, it also highlights the impact the media can have on people's emotions and their reaction to an event. The media has moved on to other events in its constant search for the current and the immediate. Yet the results of its focus on the tsunami are still being felt through each relief and rehabilitation project. The global response to the disaster was a triumph of the cyber age: events from one end of the world, digitised into words and images, travelled immediately to the other to touch the hearts of fellow human beings. Sri Lanka received a commitment of U.S. $ 2.1 billion from the international community[15].

The contributions from those living in Sri Lanka too, especially in the form of organisational and individual assistance, have been inestimable. In the immediate aftermath of the tsunami, the first 48 hours, it was the work of individuals, private sector companies, NGOs and multilateral organisations that had strong links at grassroots level in Sri Lanka that averted a major humanitarian catastrophe. Organisations in the private sector, unhampered by bureaucracy and possessing the logistics required, played a significant role in collecting and transporting aid items at their own cost to the affected areas. In turn, religious centres in each area played a key role in receiving and distributing this aid as it was brought in. Displaced people sought refuge in the temples, churches, kovils and mosques. The chief prelate of each centre took responsibility for the refugees without religious or ethnic bias and acted as the central point for coordinating the aid that was pouring into the community. Truck load after truck load of dry rations, clothes and water would be brought in and handed over to the prelates who then took on the task of managing and coordinating the distribution of the goods throughout the region.

The State needed time to comprehend the disaster and mobilise forces for large-scale relief. Many international relief agencies predicted the possibility of a second disaster through the outbreak of epidemics, while they grappled to comprehend the scale of the disaster and the coordination and strategy required to deal with it. Ultimately it was the small gifts; the heaps of clothes, the packs of cooked food, the bottles of water; those given from the heart from one individual to another, from a community to an individual or organisation they felt was capable of "doing something", that added up to create a net of relief that prevented the immediate descent into darkness. No amount of planning and strategy, at State or macro-levels, would have achieved what a culture and a people steeped in a tradition of "giving" and "serving the community" prevented in the first few hours after the tsunami in Sri Lanka.

Now, two years later, the region has moved from relief to the rehabilitation stage. Still today, it is the projects that work closely with the region, have grown out of requests by the community and have the active participation of different stakeholders of the community, that appear to hold lasting value to people affected by the tsunami.

I meet Franz Meyer two years later.[16] He tells me that the *Buckingham Tsunami Relief Tangalle District Hospital Trust,* as the project came to be known with Nick Buckingham as the Managing Trustee, is nearing completion. Nick Buckingham underwrote the project for 45,000 pounds sterling and pledged 5000 pounds of his own money. The 650,000 pounds that came in later were made up of contributions by people who were either affected by the tsunami or who heard about the project through Nick's extensive networks and connections. The local community too responded with appreciation when they saw the immense value of the reconstruction work. They contributed through their own fundraising events. A musical concert was held in Tangalle as a fundraiser with some of Sri Lanka's leading singers performing free of charge. From the initial idea of renovating a ward, the project grew into one of the largest tsunami relief initiatives in the country to be backed by an individual.

The board describing the Project is at the entrance to the Tangalle Hospital. The wall that it has been nailed onto conveys the state of the rest of the hospital before the project began.

The Buckingham Tsunami Relief Project did not stop at simply upgrading the structure of the hospital. It provided the details such as surgical attire and specialised equipment that were essential for medical procedures.

BTR
TANGALLE DISTRICT HOSPITAL TRUST
+improving this hospital+

Funds are being raised through private donations and work is taking place, in an international effort to make this a better hospital for the people of Tangalle District.

We are renovating:

- The Operating Theatre, Blood Bank, all Wards, Mortuary, Kitchen, Outpatient building,
- Also-Providing new bathroom & toilet facilities throughout the hospital
- Building and equipping a brand-new Laundry and improving the Water System
- Purchasing brand-new Medical Equipment, Beds, Mattresses and Sheets, in Sri Lanka

We expect the final project cost to be approx. Rs80,000,000 (80million) and take about 1 year. Trustees and group members work entirely for free -and do this in memory of those who died and the many who lost so much at the time of the Tsunami on December 26th 2004.

For more information please call in to see us or, telephone:047-2241213 (Monday-Saturday)
Email: btrtdhtrust @ sltnet.lk Website: www.tangallehospital.com
Buckingham Tsunami Relief TANGALLE DISTRICT HOSPITAL TRUST

POWERED BY
LTU
INTERNATIONAL AIRWAYS

Today, what was once the 'punishment hospital', where inexperienced or unmotivated staff were transferred, has been elevated to 'base hospital' status by the Ministry of Health. It is one of the best equipped hospitals in the South. It has modern wards, an up-to-date operating theatre suite with an intensive care unit, a new blood bank, a morgue, a slick kitchen, a hospital incinerator, a machine-operated laundry and a labour room with two premature baby incubators. When the project finished renovating and modernising a unit, it was handed back to the hospital staff. Then the team moved on to another unit.[17] Section by section, the project transformed the entire hospital. The hospital now not only attracts experienced doctors, but more importantly, it is also drawing in patients who would have previously had to travel miles out of the region in search of good medical facilities.

Franz tells me that the administration costs were less than 2% of the total budget and that they worked six days of the week for almost two years. He adds that it's hard to get things done here, in Sri Lanka, where things do not 'flow easily' because logistics and individuals can create frustrating blocks. He describes the labour contracts they developed, the scrupulous accounting and transparency procedures they adhered to and the trips back and forth by bus to Colombo as they purchased new equipment from suppliers and cleared goods from Customs. Listening to Franz I realise that both he and Nick Buckingham have given two years of their lives to the project.

The hands-on approach of the *Buckingham Tsunami Relief Tangalle Hospital Project* stands in direct contrast to the projects run by some international non governmental organisations. Many of these organisations rented buildings above market prices in areas where they were working and created artificial rates in the real estate sector. They opened project offices, filled them with electronic equipment and duty free vehicles; spent their budget on relocation costs, salaries and offshore benefits of expatriate staff, and brought in local staff on salaries they will not receive in another job once the project is completed. The feeling among the community is that the tsunami money meant for them is not being used fairly by some international aid agencies and charities. As a result, there is a tangible animosity among the locals towards them. In cases where faith-based organisations have tied religious conversion of individuals to the decision of 'who receives funding', this communal animosity has, at times, spilled over into open violence.

As the *Financial Times Deutschland* writes[18]:

> One lesson is clear: we humans really can be quite generous when catastrophe strikes. Some $10 billion was donated in the wake of the tsunami, and a large chunk of that came from private donations from people around the globe. But what, a number of papers are wondering on Tuesday, became of all that money (sic)?

The Financial Times Deutschland argues that the huge sum of money earmarked for the region was too much of a good thing. A number of the regions receiving the aid were not even capable of absorbing so much generosity, the paper writes.[19]....The left-leaning daily Die Tageszeitung likewise casts about for lessons learned from the world's overwhelming response to the tsunami tragedy. The first lesson is a positive one: Today's capitalist, money-hungry society is still capable of political engagement. But the use of tsunami aid money shows, the paper writes, how quickly well-intended charity can be misused. "All too often, aid workers are guided by the expectations of the public back home, which would rather donate for orphanages and fishing boats instead of funding reconstruction work determined by the locals."

The Tangalle Project is appreciated by the community for it stands at the other end of the spectrum from the approach of large relief projects. For them, the project has given them a gift that has transformed, forever, the quality of healthcare that they receive. To do so, it has taken the approach of working close to the community and its needs.

In fact, many of the projects funded by donors from overseas that have had a strong impact on recipients stem from the links foreign nationals had to local communities. Travellers who had once trekked Sri Lanka, school kids who had visited on sports tours and exchange programmes, interns and the single man or woman who had once lived in a hut on the beach: all these people who had kept a special place for Sri Lanka in their hearts have made remarkable contributions to the tsunami affected areas by spearheading fundraising projects in their communities back home. In Hambantota alone there are several ongoing programmes that have been funded by groups of individuals and communities from Norway, Canada, UK, Australia, Germany, Taiwan, France and Belgium. For instance, *Manchester Enterprises*[20], the economic development agency for Greater Manchester in UK, sent representatives to Sri Lanka after the tsunami to identify projects that could be funded by the organisation. Today, the projects developed in Hambantota through the HDCC's partnership with *Manchester Enterprises* have gone beyond relief work to focus on larger issues that affect the region such as human resource development, tourism promotion, IT development and the necessity for an organisation like the HDCC to develop its capacity as a regional chamber. As a result there have been several staff exchanges with sector-advisors in tourism, IT & youth development travelling from Manchester to Hambantota, and many HDCC staff moving to Manchester for training. All the tsunami projects that have been initiated by people and organisations from overseas are no longer simply gifts or donations from one individual or community to another; they have instead become the basis for cultural exchanges and lasting friendships between people from two different nations.

For the people of an area that is receiving tsunami aid all that seems to matter is this: from the beginning to the end, a project should account for itself through activities that are unambiguous in its genuine dedication to the welfare and the needs of the beneficiaries. They immediately recognise the projects that will do this.

Releasing
the Dead

AT THE BEGINNING of the last century, Leonard Woolf, the British Assistant Government Agent(AGA) for Hambantota, battled the inevitable administrative challenges that beset the region. An outbreak of rinderpest in 1912 brought immense hardship to the farmers who depended on cattle for their livelihood and nutrition. The occasional crisis was underlined by recurrent disasters that were an inevitable part of life in the dry zone. Malaria was endemic. Months of drought would destroy a year's cultivation by the farmers.

For Woolf, finding administrative solutions to the poverty, sickness and the general desolateness of the people's lives was a personal quest. He managed minor crises, listened to petty squabbles between the villagers and in a hundred other ways served his colonial government. Yet, the role of even an intelligent and sensitive British Assistant Government Agent was minor and his effectiveness left only a superficial mark on a region where nature had a life and a force of its own.

The purpose of the Government Agent, now officially known as the District Secretary, but called the "*GA*" by the people, has changed little over the centuries. However, unlike Woolf's solitary life where administrative decisions lay largely in his hands, today's GA is a person caught within a greater politically driven bureaucracy. For most part, the life of a GA, is one of ensuring the bureaucracy functions without disruption at one level while on another it is about juggling changing political agendas. All the while, he also grapples with two sets of administrative structures: those of the Centralised and Provincial Governments.

Mr. Piyasena was the Government Agent for Hambantota at the time of the tsunami. Hambantota was his first appointment as a GA and he had begun work two months before. His family lives in Matara. The South is his home. We meet on a Sunday evening on a paved walkway that separates the winding A2 from the sea. Across the road lies the bustle of the Matara Town; behind us is a bus-stand used by a constant stream of people travelling out of the South or further deep into it. Surrounding the bus-stand are shops and open areas with hundreds of people milling around. On the 26th, the road behind us had been inaccessible. The bus-stand and most of the Town had been destroyed.

Mr. Piyasena had made his way to Hambantota from his home in Matara on the back-roads. He had gone to the closest hospital; the Tangalle Hospital which had not been affected by the waves but was by then teeming with the injured and the dying. He describes to me the decisions made by the District Medical Officer (DMO) and himself, "The DMO and I talked about how we could issue the dead bodies to the families claiming them. Many of the people here are Muslims and we had to issue the bodies to the families to perform the burial rites within 24 hours. And anyway, this is a tropical country we had no place to keep so many bodies. By that time we had over 60 bodies inside the hospital."

The DMO and Mr. Piyasena had agreed to by-pass the lengthy process involved in issuing a death certificate, particularly the requirement for an autopsy. They had decided on one thing (a stroke of administrative brilliance given the chaos they were working within), that a photograph would be taken of each corpse released to a claimant. On the first day alone the Tangalle Hospital had released over 68 bodies. He gives me the final statistics for Hambantota, and it is clear he has had to repeat these many times. The number of corpses recovered was 3068. Incidentally, they had used over 30 rolls of photographic film most of which had been brought in from Ratnapura when stocks had run out in Hambantota.

The tsunami crisis took place on a public holiday when all banks and government institutions were closed. Their staff were also affected by the disaster. Electricity cables and telephone lines were damaged, and the water supply was polluted with sea water and

UN Secretary General, Kofi Annan and Mrs. Annan with President Mahinda Rajapakse and Azmi Thassim in Hambantota during their tour of tsunami affected areas in Sri Lanka.

debris. The immediate need was for food, water and shelter. Yet the coastal road from Colombo, the A2, was impassable, making it difficult for supplies to be brought in from outside the region. Mr. Piyasena had borrowed the cash available in-hand with the heads of other Government agencies in the District. He tells me how he got about Rs. 20,000 from different departments and government offices in Hambantota to purchase dry rations and prepare food for the displaced on the first night.

The current President, Mahinda Rajapaksa was the Prime Minister in 2004 and the President was not in Sri Lanka at the time of the tsunami. The Prime Minister managed the crisis until the President returned to Sri Lanka and took over the relief operations a few days later. By mid afternoon on the 26th Mahinda Rajapaksa had flown in to Hambantota. He had given Mr. Piyasena and his team of administrators the authority to use the emergency money available to him and to make any decisions necessary to handle the crisis. Mr. Piyasena therefore received an important impetus to dealing with the crisis; the backing from the very top ranks of government.

The disruption created by the tsunami was unique. For the first time, although briefly, religious, ethnic and social differences ceased to matter, and people related to one another with an acute awareness that the only link that counted, once all else had been destroyed, was the common bond of being human. The very nature of the chaos the tsunami wrought and the complete isolation and inaccessibility it caused also had the power to create a suspension of all the petty human agendas that manifest through the socio-political machinery. The lashing from nature destabilised and overturned all existing physical and administrative structures and systems that usually hold society together. The result of the immediate aftermath of the tsunami was therefore a space in-between this lashing, and the human effort to bring back the order and the systems that contain society and individual lives within a manageable and controllable setting. This was the space that allowed actions

of selfless courage and human generosity. It was a space that suspended a person's ethnic or religious affiliations. But it was also a place where greatness was contrasted against human greed through actions such as looting, theft and murder. In its essence, however, this was a space where only the human spirit could have tipped the balance, and during the first few weeks following the tsunami in Sri Lanka, the best of human nature came to the surface and triumphed.

Mr. Piyasena is a person who has glimpsed the opening of that brief in-between space and had seen people in action within it. Yet, when the machinery of the Government had slowly filtered in, he had gone back to his role with the perfect understanding that the closing of that space was inevitable.

"And there were the mad things that also happen at times like these. You know, we are here trying to deal with this, and we get requests from Colombo for numbers and reports of how many bodies are coming in, how many houses were damaged," Mr. Piyasena chuckles to himself.

Mr. Piyasena meets his team at the beginning of another day in the District Secretariat.

Loss

THERE ARE HUNDREDS of blogs and emails circulating on the internet for information on people missing from the tsunami. As late as November 2006, the occasional news clip appears in the papers when relatives send out a search for a lost family member. National authorities call for families of surviving children who are presumed to have been separated from their parents during the tsunami. Several children have been found after the tsunami with families that *"could not produce any documentary evidence to prove a child's parentage"*[21]. The newspapers carry photographs of wide-eyed children, some less than three years old. Some of the photos are the most recent image the family has of the child before he or she went missing in the tsunami. Even in those, which are badly reproduced in the newspaper, the image seems distant and out of date.

Coping with the loss of a loved one has been most difficult for a survivor when no remains of the lost person were found. The sense of finality that comes with death has been prevented by the hope the person may be found, as some were, through luck and weird twists of fate. There are the stories of the infant who was lifted off in a plastic pail by the waves to be later found lodged, unscathed, in the branches of a tree, or the man who regained his memory weeks later and wandered back searching for his family. Yet these are outweighed by heartrending tales of survivors who are still searching and waiting for the appearance of even one loved one.

The national impact of the tsunami, given the scale of the disaster, on the mental health of the people in Sri Lanka is yet to be studied. In Aceh, a survey by *Medecins sans Frontiers* conducted in July 2005, estimated that 83% of people showed signs of severe emotional distress and 77% had symptoms of depression[22]. Dr. Mahoney, World Health

Organisation Consultant on mental health and social issues in Sri Lanka during 2005 said, "'We know that around 5% of people who live through such an experience will develop mental health problems - so around 25,000 people were likely to have been affected. . . . But he said, people coping with the aftermath of the tsunami were not offered psychiatric services or counselling if they were experiencing understandable stress or anxiety as a result of losing their home or their livelihood.'"[23]

A minority of professionals in the field have questioned the appropriateness of some of the services offered. As Carolyn Rayn reports:

> Dr. Derek Summerfield, a psychiatrist at the Maudsley Hospital in London, who has worked in Bosnia and in the hotspots of Israel, among other areas, says there is a tendency after wars and disasters to see anxiety and stress problems where they may not exist - or to conclude people have not realised how they have been affected.
>
> One expert said children in a village he was visiting were smiling and happy, and just wanted to get back to school. He described them as 'clearly in denial'.
>
> He added: "We have exported to this part of the world the assumption that something so atrocious that there must have been some kind of mental health effect (sic).
>
> But what people are asking for was not mental health care. It was help repairing homes and schools.
>
> Dr. Summerfield said there would be some people who did experience mental health problems because of their tsunami experience, but that the number would be "tiny". [24]

In Sri Lanka too several leading clinical psychologists have stressed that most people could be cared for within the community by the existing social networks that have traditionally provided support to individuals in times of crisis throughout their lives. They comment that community leaders, religious leaders, personal confidants, informal networks and cultural rituals for grieving seem more viable and appropriate means for mental healthcare in this country. Particularly, as 'counselling' and 'therapy' delivered by inadequately trained staff without a long-term professional commitment to the patient and to follow-up care could cause real harm to the recovery process of the individual.

In a country where there are only 38 psychiatrists, 17 occupational therapists and 420 psychiatric nurses for a total population of 20 million people[25] it is probably community care and a culturally conditioned response to tragedy that sustained survivors of the tsunami. Also, local groups in each town such as the *Trader's Association of Hambantota Town,* in Hambantota organised ceremonies that brought the community together to mourn the loss and commemorate the dead. The efforts of such local organisations were always driven from within the community: the funds, the ideas, and the labour for the preparation of food, for instance, were contributed by the people from the area. They took ownership of both the event and its results. Driven by the satisfaction of having organised a successful event, the associations have added these programmes to their annual calendar of events. Therefore, such ceremonies have created a shared space for individuals to mourn their loss and bereavement over an extended period of time within familiar boundaries.

Also, the tsunami was not selective in its devastation. It lashed into people's lives with no regard for a person's educational background, ethnicity or place on the social ladder. Society was levelled. One of the survivors in Hambantota made a very pertinent comment: *"See, everybody lost something. No one was alone in that sense, and there seemed to be always a person who had lost more than us."*[26] Elizabeth Kübler–Ross writes on death and grieving: "If our first reaction to catastrophic news is, 'No, it's not true, no it cannot involve me,' this has to give way to a new reaction, when it finally dawns on us: 'Oh, yes, it was me, it was not a mistake.'....The logical next question becomes: Why me?"[27] In coastal

communities such as Hambantota, the question was "why us?" The personal experience was transferred into a collective one and the pain of loss was shared by those around the survivor not as empathisers but as victims themselves. Also, in Sri Lanka people have lived with the stress of war for decades and have therefore been forced to develop coping mechanisms that those living in a different cultural setting would only find through professional care. As psychiatrist, Dr. Howard C. Cutler comments:

> Although pain and suffering are experienced by all human beings, I have often felt those brought up in some Eastern cultures appear to have a greater acceptance and tolerance of suffering. Part of this may be due to their beliefs, but perhaps it is because suffering is more visible in poorer nations such as India than it is in wealthier countries. Hunger, poverty, illness and death are in plain view. ..... Those living in daily contact with the realities of life cannot easily deny that life is characterized by suffering, that it is a natural part of existence.[28]

It was perhaps this culture of community service, individual resilience, an acceptance of suffering and the nature of mass loss that enabled people to move forward with their lives after the tsunami. The overwhelming sense in each community and most individuals is one of coming to terms with the loss. Today, people are looking to the future.

Women sit under a 'bo tree' in a temple as a Buddhist priest guides them through a puja.

Reviving an Industry

Most of the boats in the harbour are new: all donations made by charities to the fishermen after the tsunami.

THE FISHING INDUSTRY in Sri Lanka produced 300,000 metric tonnes of fish annually[29]. In a few hours the tsunami reduced most of the industry to rubble. Almost the entire shipping fleet was rendered useless. Storage rooms were destroyed and the personal lives of people who were part of the industry were disrupted and lost. The *Asian Development Bank* estimates that the sector employed 142,500 fishermen and that prior to the tsunami there were 29,700 boats in operation. It is believed that a total 27,000 fishermen and their family members died in the tsunami.[30] In Hambantota alone, approximately 1000 fishing boats were reported damaged and the infrastructure and equipment that supported the industry such as ice storages, nets, repair workshops and equipment were destroyed.

Restoring the industry was a challenge. Reconstruction appeared to be a long drawn-out process that would take several years. The real difficulty, however, came from the complete informality of the sector. The fishing industry in Sri Lanka is not regulated. There are no procedures to document invaluable data such as the number of boats, active fishermen, their markets and production capacities in one cohesive system. The industry operates through ad-hoc village level co-operatives, independent merchants, private associations, non governmental organisations and an authoritative body established by the Government. This disparateness of the industry, coupled with the industry being viewed by donors as one of easiest entry points for rebuilding the economic livelihoods of survivors, caused a reconstruction disaster in the industry after the tsunami. According to Steve Creech, Consultant in Fisheries,[31] crisis management and emergency relief were confused

with rehabilitation and reconstruction by many donors. Relief projects were uncoordinated in regions and between agencies. Many donors and organisations began providing boats and equipment to the surviving fishermen before the industry had rebuilt the infrastructure that was necessary to support it. Some of the boats provided were inappropriate for local conditions and fishing capacity. Many received duplicates as there was no coordination between the donors. There was no means of cross-checking whether a recipient had received a boat before. Some fishermen were unable to access any boats.

A large local institution, for instance, having received funds from donors for tsunami relief work, used the money to purchase a fleet of boats. The boats were purchased without consulting the recipients and without correct technical advice on the type of vessel suited to the local marine environment or fishing capacities. The boats were distributed to fishermen in Hambantota. The institution had neither the capacity nor the inclination to monitor and evaluate the impact of the donation on the community over a period of time. The 'gift', however, continues to have enormous repercussions on the Hambantota fishing community even today. The fishermen soon realised that the boats were not appropriate for the local environment and were forced to discard them. Many missed the opportunity to access boats from other donors and have been without a fishing vessel for two years. Mercifully, the original donors remain unaware of the ineffectual use of their funds. The institution however, will no doubt record the 'gift' in its annual report as an example of the successful fulfilment of its 'corporate responsibility' towards society.

One of the indirect causes for the initial delay in the recovery came from the sudden decline in the consumption of seafood. Rumours spread that fish was contaminated by debris and human carcasses in the ocean. Despite repeated efforts by the government and other organisations to allay these fears by citing research findings, the fish consuming public took their time returning to seafood.[32]

The fishing industry took over a year to reach a stage of recovery to operate at pre-tsunami capacity. And many of the reconstruction projects to develop harbours and industry facilities in line with longer-term development plans for the coastal region are now in progress.

Transforming Hambantota

AZMI THASSIM shows me his parents' house in Hambantota Town. The doors and windows of the house have been shuttered with planks. Most of the building has been damaged; the plaster stripped and the roof disjointed by the water. Azmi points to an area of the house and tells me that had he stayed in Hambantota on the 26th of December, he would have been in "that room" when the tsunami came in. It faces the A2 main highway. Across the road is an expanse of land that runs up to the beach. On the roadside edge of this land is a line of shops and behind it had once been houses. At the furthest end, almost on the beach, was the Sunday market. This area was devastated by the tsunami. It recorded the highest number of deaths in Hambantota when the waves swept away people who had come to the market, those living in the houses and those working in the shops close by. Some of the people who survived were found about a kilometre inland among heaps of debris that the waves had carried in.

Azmi had returned to Hambantota when he heard about the devastation. What had followed were endless days and sleepless nights of working with government officials, the displaced and the bereaved. He describes how they went in search of people only to realise that many had been swept away by the water. He tells me how he sat in tractors loaded with decomposing corpses as they rushed to bury them. The waves that had taken people into the sea brought the bodies back in hundreds on to the shore. He describes the mass graves they had to dig and the religious rites they performed on their knees in the soaked fields.

Boats are moored on the beach around the Hambantota harbour until they are taken back to sea at dusk.

Azmi is the head of the Hambantota District Chamber of Commerce (HDCC). Given the vagaries of the region, an under-served periphery district of Sri Lanka, this chamber has taken on a life of its own. When it was inaugurated in 1993, the Chamber was the first of its kind outside Colombo where a group of entrepreneurs had joined forces to form an alliance to promote business within a District. The thirteen entrepreneurs, including Azmi who founded the chamber, were from the region and understood its issues and the its people. The HDCC was a groundbreaking venture given not only the District it sprang from but also the circumstances that compelled the entrepreneurs to form it.

In 1971 and in the last years of the 1980's the Southern region was the base of a national level insurrection. Triggered by unemployment, poverty and discrimination by a centralised State government, the events of '71 and '89 became synonymous with the South where inequity had bred turmoil and bitterness. A 'chamber of commerce' seemed an appropriate medium to attempt an economic regeneration when the State had struggled to deliver a suitable solution to this crisis. Today the HDCC has hundreds of members, has been instrumental in creating opportunities for families to start cottage enterprises, has helped with job placement for youth and inaugurated large-scale business projects to pave the way for economic regeneration in the area. The HDCC now has a wide network of links within the country as well as globally. One such link has been the *Youth Business International*[33] partnership, a programme of the *International Business Leaders Forum* set up by the Prince of Wales, that helps disadvantaged youth realise their potential as entrepreneurs.

The HDCC is an example of the efforts of a small group of people who have been trying to break the isolation of Hambantota from the rest of the country. These people have been attempting to give the District the structural and economic backing that will enable it to compete with the rest of the country in areas of trade, commerce and human resources. They consider themselves *people of the South*. Individuals from the *South* such as the President of Sri Lanka, Mahinda Rajapaksa, Azmi Thassim, and Chamal Rajapaksa, who are involved in this effort, have one thing in common. They carry with them a knowing that this *South* is their life. They may live outside it, in Colombo and in other parts of the world from time to time, but the *South* never leaves them. This sense of place that they carry in their blood permeates their worldview. To Azmi, Colombo will always be made up of "them": his vision will be towards Hambantota. These are people who have made the success of this region their personal mission. At the end of every professional meeting and interaction he has outside Hambantota, seems to hang the question, "What can this person; this situation do for us?" This vision has been the redeeming grace of the South. It is a vision that rises above personal gain and looks towards a larger success that all communities and people could benefit from. Without these individuals, the South would indeed be left behind.

For people such as Azmi, the tsunami was a double tragedy. It overturned their personal lives and it destroyed the entire economic foundation they had been building for the regeneration they wanted to create in Hambantota. Decades of work and hope were lost. The journey of reviving the South is now longer than it has ever been.

Nevertheless, the reconstruction of local economies of regions affected by the tsunami such as Hambantota has begun and many businesses that were devastated by the tsunami have received support through the financial assistance allocated by donors for small and medium scale enterprises. Countries such as Norway, Sweden, the U.S.A., Japan, Netherlands and the U.K. pledged funds to local organisations for distribution to suitable recipients. The entrepreneurs therefore received an enormous boost as they set about re-building their businesses. They were able to construct new buildings and upgrade their enterprises to a level above their standard before the tsunami. According to Mr. Ramanayake[34], Operations Manager of HDCC, by the end of April 2005, the HDCC had received 212 requests for funds from small and medium businesses that had been affected by the tsunami. By 2007, the total requests for assistance had increased to 2500 and the HDCC had supported over 1800 of the total requests, capturing 80% of the affected

Azmi Thassim's house
is yet to be renovated.
A neighbour was saved
from death when the tsu-
nami waves lifted him off
his balcony and deposited
him inside the water-
tank that rises above
the walls of the house.

59

businesses in Hambantota. The aid for these projects had been granted by the *Royal Norwegian Embassy*, the *Ceylon Chamber of Commerce*, the *Federation of Chambers of Commerce and Industry of Sri Lanka, Mercy Corps and the Asia Foundation,* using which, the HDCC had mobilised a large network of staff and monitoring processes to disburse the funds. The donors' approach of working through organisations such as the HDCC, which had strong links to the local community, ensured that grants were distributed to genuine recipients and allowed for continuous monitoring and evaluation of the utilisation of the funds by the grantees. Also, the management of donor aid required a number of skilled and dedicated staff within local organisations. This, in turn, created employment opportunities for local youth. The HDCC for instance had hired 13 new employees for the tsunami projects.

As I spend time in Hambantota I visit the new projects that have come up: the Tangalle District Hospital, the school in Kirinda that is being renovated and the housing estates that cover vast tracts of land. The Ministries of Education and Health have signed Memoranda of Understanding with multilateral organisations such as UNICEF and UNFPA, with UNOPS as a technical partner, to develop schools and health facilities. In Hambantota alone, this project is now in the process of reconstructing 8 health facilities and 7 schools which will be completed in 2007.[35] All these projects have strengthened the infrastructure of a region which would otherwise have been overlooked. The changes have been however not only structural. Very briefly, post-tsunami working committees demonstrated that alternative ways of interaction and decision making, not led by personal agendas, were possible when a group gathered to achieve a common objective. For instance in Hambantota, representatives from all political parties, religious organisations and other stakeholding groups, came together as one 'committee' to plan the tsunami reconstruction projects for the Hambantota Town. This group, which was made up of individuals with very different political and personal agendas, functioned together with success as the 'committee' sought to find common solutions to post-tsunami challenges. The success of such a 'committee' remains an example of the consensus that can be arrived at when there are individuals willing to engage in such an exercise. For Azmi these are all the positive results of the tragedy.

Yet Azmi has a clear understanding that the changes to the region and the people's lives which were catalysed by the tsunami could be superficial: they have been brought about artificially and too soon. He questions their validity and ability to be sustained in the long term. He wonders what alternatives there could be if this phase of reconstruction is to be taken as an opportunity for growth and whether everything will return to the former equilibrium once the funding shifts elsewhere. The answers will need to be found by the people of the South, who understand it best and who live there day in and day out.

Changing Landscapes

LEONARD WOOLF based his novel, *The Village in the Jungle,* on Hambantota. While the characters and the events in the novel are fictitious, the geographical setting and the way of life that Woolf captured were real:

> All jungles are evil, but no jungle is more evil than that which lay about the village of Beddagama. If you climb one of the rocks that jut up out of it, you will see the jungle stretched out below you for mile upon mile on all sides. It looks like a great sea, over which the pitiless hot wind perpetually sends waves unbroken, except where the bare rocks, rising above it, show like dark smudges against the grey green of the leaves. For ten months of the year the sun beats down and scorches it; and hot wind in a whirl of dust tears over it, tossing the branches and scattering the leaves. The trees are stunted and twisted by the drought, by the thin and sandy soil, by the dry wind.[36]

Even today, while much of the landscape in the interior of Hambantota has changed since the beginning of the last century, the essence of the dry zone jungle that makes up the region remains the same. Most of Hambantota is made up of nature reserve, and even where people have moved out towards the more habitable eastern regions, the battle with the jungle is a part of these inhabitant's lives. The weather and the wildlife always threaten to creep in and destroy the world built by humans. Elephants that roam the reserves such as Yala encroach upon the settlements in search of food and water. The drought and the months of endless arid weather make the place exceedingly dusty. The dust covers every inch of every surface. The landscape and the weather define the patterns of habitation and distribution of the population. Michael York Smith writes, "...the people are not spread evenly over the district and are found in much greater concentration in the wetter, Western parts."[37]

After the tsunami, the government allocated land for housing projects without taking into consideration the impact of these settlements on the environment or on the lifestyles of the residents for whom they were intended. Consequently, vast tracts of land which were previously jungle, the roaming grounds of elephants and other fauna, have been cleared for the construction of new houses. The tsunami damaged over 2300 houses in Hambantota. By 2005, the Task Force for Rebuilding the Nation (TAFREN)[38] records that Memoranda of Understanding had been signed by the government and various donors for the construction of over 4187 houses in Hambantota. The number of houses scheduled for construction exceeds the number damaged as the allocations have not been per house damaged but by family unit. Traditionally several families, spanning as many as three generations, lived in one building, but now, every family that lived in areas affected by the waves have had access to a separate home.

The area named *Siribopura*, where hundreds of acres of State land have been allocated for new settlements as part of the 130,000 hectare *Ruhunupura* development project, is a sea of roofs in many shapes and sizes. Row after row of houses rise from the red ground like from a *Monopoly* board game that has gone berserk. Already the estate has over 1602 completed houses funded by individuals, communities and organisations. The *Tzu Chi Foundation's* housing project is one of the few tsunami projects that has been exemplary in its long-term commitment to the project and the welfare of the recipients. The Foundation has built hundreds of houses taking into account individual and cultural lifestyle needs, has looked into the needs of the housing scheme as a communal unit and has made a long term, five year, commitment to the project with project representatives on-site to deal with

OVERLEAF

Slowly, with more rain, the landscape will come back to life for a brief interlude from the incessant drought.

issues. This approach however, is the exception. Most of the housing projects have been built with little planning or any attempt to create a cohesive living environment centred around the needs of the inhabitants.

Yet, people are doing their best to settle into the new housing estates. Most of the houses are occupied. However, many families still live in two places: in the new house and in a place closer to where their previous residence used to be for the convenience of accessing schools, hospitals and their source of livelihood. There is however, an air of willingness to look to the future, an acknowledgement that a house symbolises the possibility of a new beginning that is essential for those who have encountered traumatic loss. This has made people keen to make the adjustments that the move to the new homes have called for. They seem willing to bear the frustrations of bad planning that has not considered issues such as water and garbage disposal and to adapt to insensitive architecture that has not taken cultural or religious backgrounds of the occupants into account.

However, overriding all the adjustments that the housing estates call for and the people's willingness to adapt is the grip the landscape and the weather have on the ultimate success or failure of the new communities. Previous settlements in the Eastern parts of Hambantota were small; they encroached upon the jungle in occasional bouts and allowed for the sustenance that came from the natural world with its ground cover and redeeming shade of the sparse growth of trees. The new settlements do not offer this relief. They have cleared acres of jungle for housing estates and bared the land, exposing inhabitants to the aridity that is the underlying bane of Hambantota. The sun remains merciless. The dust is all pervading and settles in thick heaps as the scrub that once covered the ground has been removed. Wells run dry. Nothing grows.

This is the second battle between nature and a people who survived their first with the tsunami. Here too, if necessary, they would survive. Yet, the question they will finally ask of themselves about their lives in the new estates is whether it is necessary to struggle when an option remains to return to areas that are less harsh for human habitation. In time, the people will decide.

It has taken several
weeks of monsoon rain
to give the housing estate
this touch of greenery.

The following pages profile a group of people in Hambantota as they describe their memories of the tsunami and their lives today...

68

The 'neighbourhood kids' who used the beach as their playground were among the first to return to the beach once the debris left behind by the tsunami was cleared.

The Conch Shell Collection

A WOMAN draped in a cotton sari comes to the entrance of her home to greet me. As she bustles towards us she lifts the edge of her sari to drape it over her head. I look at her and think she must be around 30 years, but her laughter, open smile and figure gives her the playfulness of a teenager.

Her house, in which we are sitting, is new. It's one in an estate of houses that has been built after the tsunami. Rizvana has filled the living room with a few plastic chairs for the guests, and on a table at the far end there is a brand new television, and a DVD player. The new curtains on the windows are of expensive fabric. They rise and fall over our heads, battling the breeze that seems to blow straight from the sea, even though the new houses are set back from the beach.

Rizvana stands against the wall closest to me and starts talking about the day the tsunami came into her village:

"Suddenly people were running away, shouting that the sea was coming. My brother came by, telling us to go away so I sent the two boys with him. Then I went to the gate to look out for my husband. And then the water started filling up."

She describes how her husband returned soon after and they began their flight from the water. "We started climbing over the walls and we had the next door neighbour's daughter and the old woman who helped me in the house to take with us. But the old woman went. The wall broke as we climbed and it fell on us. . .but at the same time the waves took the wall away. We all swam and swam and managed to get to the ground where everybody had escaped to."

As she talks, her husband walks into the house. Hansan is 35 years old and, in complete contrast to Rizvana, has a look of perpetual disenchantment on his face. He listens to his wife's banter.

"Imagine lifting her over the wall. And there was another one from next door too. I couldn't take them all, so the old woman went," he shrugs. I try to draw out from him if she died or they simply lost her from the group. "They found her washed ashore later. About two miles from here," he says.

Hansan goes on to tell me how the tsunami has affected him. He separates himself from people who had 'nothing' before the tsunami and stood only to gain from the donations they received in the form of a house and land. "It's ok for them, but I lost about 5 lakhs worth of conch shells and everything else, the fridge, the television, the set-up. For us it is different," he says and purses his mouth. Bitterness fills the room.

Conch shells are collected from the bottom of the sea by divers and then re-sold for export to Bangladesh where the shells are polished and turned into jewellery. Hansan had just begun this venture on top of his day-job at the government-owned salterns. A day of harvesting costs a large sum of money for a man whose monthly salary is around $50. The costs of hiring the boat, paying the divers and food for the crew alone come to more than $50 and Hansan had just been breaking even with his costs when the tsunami struck. Now, with a life to pick up, the instalments for the new television, DVD and costs of furnishing a house, he says he can't think of organising a trip for shell harvesting. He describes the pit he had built to store the shells. The entire store had emptied with the water. I understand the look of disenchantment on his face.

Hansan pauses for a few seconds and adds, "And every month I have to take her to the doctor about the headaches she gets. The medicine is very expensive." Hansan describes the intense headaches that Rizvana has been suffering from since the tsunami. Rizvana smiles self-consciously and nods in agreement.

"When we got to high ground we heard that our eldest son had gone missing," says

Rizvana. Her ebullience suddenly appears to be only a thin shell covering up the trauma caused by the tsunami. For a brief moment she stops smiling.

"But we found him later. Someone had put him on a bus and he was taken to the police station," Rizvana says, and laughs.

The School Master

OUTSIDE MR. ASSAR'S house, along the boundary of the garden, is a small makeshift nursery of plants. Several rows of young vines have been planted in the front garden sheltered under a roof of transparent polythene. This is early September; the rains are still to arrive in Kirinde. The wind is severe and the sun relentless. Yet the small plants in Mr. Assar's garden are lush and green. They have been well looked after and watered regularly. The plants reflect a gardener who is tending them with much hope pinned on them.

Mr. Assar lives in the same housing estate as Rizvana and Hansan. The house is identical to the one I had sat in a few hours ago listening to Rizvana's banter and Hansan's wry comments. Mr. Assar sits in the living room while his three year-old granddaughter toddles around the room looking at the strangers who have invaded her house. He tells me of the day the tsunami struck.

"This child was only a few months," he says, pointing to the toddler. Mr. Assar remembers a wall breaking on him from the impact of the water and then he had blacked out. When he recovered, he had found himself alone and injured. His first thought had been of his family and he had gone looking for them. After hours of searching he had found his wife who had been taken into the sea but had been rescued by a group of young men. He tells me that because of them, many people who would have otherwise died, escaped. They had then begun the search for their daughters.

Mr. Assar stands next to
the vegetable saplings
that he has grown in
plastic bags which will
be replanted in plots
when the rains arrive.

One of them had been taken to higher ground by Rizvana and Hansan. I realise then that they had been neighbours and this was the other person that Hansan had helped. I remembered Hansan's words, "I couldn't help them all." The life of Mr. Assar's daughter was saved.

The search for the second daughter had taken them out of Kirinda to Badulla, a town over 130 kilometres from Kirinda. This is not an easy journey as it is a relentless uphill climb. Yet Badulla has a large hospital and when the A2 road became impassable and therefore the hospitals in Galle and Tangalle were inaccessible, the injured were taken inland for medical facilities. A villager had remembered seeing Mr. Assar's daughter in a truck heading out of Kirinda. With only that tenuous link to their daughter, he and his wife had gone inland. After days of searching they had found her warded in the Badulla hospital. He tells me that the whole family had stayed at the hospital and slept on the floor in the ward. They had been treated and cared for by the staff with immense kindness.

Two years later as we sit in Mr. Assar's new house it seems to me that his life is in order. His family is safe, and no one had died in the tsunami. Yet the cost of getting his life back to the way he was living before the tsunami has been inestimable.

Mr. Assar is the English teacher of the Magama Maha Vidhyalaya, the school in Magama. The school teacher holds a central place in any village. He is an individual who is respected in his community for his education and economic status. The tsunami sent all these established community based relationships into disarray. Communities were 'levelled' in a way that they could never have been by any other force or authority. People who never owned houses now have brand new ones. Multiple families that lived together, usually several generations in one house, have received a house for each family. All these houses are no different from those given to people who lived in their own houses before the tsunami; they are identical in design and extent. The houses do not come with any furnishing and equipment. Householders have the unimaginable task of re-filling their lives with the basics and luxuries that they had spent a lifetime accumulating. Therefore all the status symbols that differentiated the different social classes before the tsunami have become invalid. This is deeply disturbing to people such as Mr. Assar, when they have to re-build lives within the same community.

For most people, surviving the tsunami was a question of arbitrary choices made by others, the courage of strangers, quick thinking and above all, luck. Survival had little to do with personal control over the final outcome. Building a life after the tsunami, however, has been an ongoing effort. For some, it has become a life that calls for the courage to wake up every morning knowing that it will be another day of worrying about paying the next instalment for the television and wondering how to pay the loan for the new chairs. For a person midpoint in his life, limited by a less than a generous salary, this task is also deeply embittering.

In a few months the plants in Mr. Assar's garden will bear a good crop of several kilos of snake-gourd and pumpkin. Provided the rains come and there is no drought, he should be able to sell these at the market to supplement his income. Mr. Assar is doing all he can to re-create the life he once had.

Receiving a Family[39]

IMRAN AND REHANA are teenagers. Rehana, Imran's sister, is 16 and shows the signs of a young girl who will, overnight, transform into a beautiful young woman, taking all those around her by surprise. Imran is 14, but looks younger. They chat to me at the entrance to their home. There is a quiet seriousness about both of them that their smiles and open sprits cannot hide.

During every school vacation, Imran and his sister Rehana would leave their home in Hambantota Town to spend a few days with their mother's sister and her husband. Maleeha and Anuruddha live in a small village close to Tangalle and are both teachers at the local school. They do not have children of their own: Imran and Rehana's visits had always been much looked forward to.

Imran and Rehana had gone to their aunt's house during the holidays in December 2004 as they had done almost every year. When the tsunami waves came in that year they were at their aunt's house away from the beach. They were safe. However, before long, rumours about the chaos the waves had created in Hambantota Town had started to spread. At the heels of the rumours came the devastating news that it was unlikely anyone who lived in the area close to their home would have survived. Each message, rumour and snippet carried to them by someone who had managed to make his way through the debris had brought less and less hope that their parents would have survived. Before long it had been confirmed that their parents were missing and that there was nothing left of their home. Several days later they had gone home to find nothing left of it: not a wall or a piece of furniture. Imran and Rehana were 12 and 14 years old in 2004. Their childhood had been washed away.

Imran and Rehana have received immense warmth and love from their aunt who herself had to mourn the loss of a sister. She and her husband have taken the two siblings

A vivid painting of the day the wave came in, by Pushpika Nanayakkara, aged ten, of the Royal Institute, Nugegoda.

14" x 10". Crayon on art paper.
11/ 05/ 2005.

into their lives as the children they never had. They have entered them to the school at which they teach. They have given them the best of all material comforts they can offer. Most of all, and most importantly, they have made them feel loved and wanted in their lives.

However, there is tension between Imran and Rehana's father's family and their foster parents. Anuruddha belongs to the Sinhala community and Imran's father's family fear this would mean the siblings may not have exposure to an Islamic lifestyle. The two teenagers are caught in the cross currents of love and attachment at one end and a value system at the other. They have not made up their minds about what they need to do and whom they should live with. They have been through heartbreak and loss once and do not want another episode of it again for themselves or for their foster parents. In time, they may have to make decisions about their identities and loyalties. At the moment, however, Imran and Rehana are too busy trying to recover from the trauma of the tsunami surrounded by the love of two people who have given them a home. In turn, Maleeha and Anuruddha have received a family. They are now the parents who will be around as the two siblings make their passage to adulthood.

Life around the Bay

THE HAMBANTOTA BAY is a long stretch of scenic beach with the harbour at one end and pockets of dense settlements at the other. We drive from the stretch of beach where the market once was towards the Southern end of the Bay. Here the roads are narrow and the area had once been the home of a bustling community, but now it is almost deserted with only a few families living in the houses that were spared or only partially destroyed by the tsunami. The others who survived have moved to the new houses built on housing estates away from the sea.

The name-board behind
Mr. Premadasa informs
the public that he is a
Justice of the Peace.

This end of the Bay is also the home of one of the oldest hotels in Hambantota, *The Peacock Beach*. It is on the edge of the shore and is therefore set far back from the road. The hotel was damaged by the waves and now, two years later, it has completed reconstruction work and is about to have a formal re-launch. Through the gates that open up to a long driveway we can see painters and carpenters painstakingly putting the final touches to a wooden fence that runs along the driveway.

Further away from the hotel we pass a small guest house run by a Parliamentarian. I am told by Azmi Thassim, who is taking me around, that the owner's wife had survived because she had been swept onto the uppermost branches of a tree. He points to a tree that rises over the two storied building.

We continue down the road to visit Sumudu Mallikarachi and her husband who own a furniture shop. Sumudu stands at the entrance of a two storied building where the ground floor has been converted into a shop piled with furniture and mattresses. The upper floor is their home. Sumudu and her family had been away in December, holidaying with friends in the hill country, but she and her husband had returned as soon as they had heard about the tsunami. She points towards the balcony and says, "A district officer's car was on the balcony. And there was a body in our living room upstairs." She waves her hand towards the staircase. She is no longer looking at me, but at Azmi.

"I didn't even let my husband see it. We got the police in and I cleaned the room. The smell! It was there for days," she says and continues to look to Azmi, for this is a shared history. I am the outsider.

"My life is completely different now. Usually, at this time, I would be talking to my friends as they go to the Sunday market. All those people are now gone. My life is completely empty. I can't describe the loneliness here in this place," her eyes fill with tears.

The Peacock Beach Hotel in Hambantota was reopened in 2006.

We drive away from the bay to a school which is empty except for a few students who have come in for weekend lessons. A frail man dressed in a white sarong and shirt is sitting in a classroom with his back to the door. He does not hear us until we go round and he sees Azmi. He struggles to stand up and grabs Azmi's hand. The mutual affection between the two men is there for everyone to see.

"Mr. Premadasa was our village mail sorter," says Azmi. "He has known us from the time we were children. Mr. Premadasa used to live close to the Peacock Beach Hotel."

"I am now 80 years old."

"How are you these days?"

"If you can only help my son," says Mr. Premadasa to Azmi without answering his question. For Mr. Premadasa, Azmi is a powerful man who can make things happen. Azmi smiles enigmatically.

"Mr. Premadasa has been always doing things for the community. He is in every committee and association, but he lost his family in the tsunami."

"I went for my tea to that Muslim hotel. You know the one close to your house. I spoke to the girls who always look out for me. And then I went on my way." Mr. Premadasa starts sobbing.

"They all went you know. And then my son found me and told me not to go home. So I didn't go. He told me that everybody who was at home had gone. My wife. We were married for 50 years. My daughter and the others are all gone. Everyone in the shop is gone." He wipes his tears and his hands shake.

Speaking of his wife he says, "I was good to her. I was good to her you know. I did a lot for her family."

Later when we get up to leave, he reminds Azmi about helping his son. He grabs Azmi's hand and implores. On our way back Azmi tells me that Mr. Premadasa had been found on the road, incoherent and dazed after the tsunami. He had not recovered for many months and had lived with his daughter in Eheliyagoda, a town in the interior of the country. Now he is back in Hambantota and makes it through each day, sustained by the committees and societies he helps with.

The Fishermen

AT THE BREAK of dawn, fishing boats begin their return to the Hambantota harbour with the night's catch. By mid morning, most of the boats have anchored. As the catch is unloaded, an industry goes into motion. If you drive down any of the roads leading to the beach near the harbour in Hambantota Town you will find yourself thrown into the bustle of the fishing industry at its peak. Pails of *sprats* are poured into regi-foam boxes layered with chunks of ice, and whole carcasses of tuna, seer, shark are stacked into vans. Fresh blood stains the puddled ground and thousands of clear, unblinking eyes stare at the sky. Men sort the fish, separating the catch for the local markets and for distribution to Colombo and other towns throughout the country. The vendors make their purchases while the fisher-merchants supervise the day's catch.

On the 26th morning, S.N. Shihabi and two other fishermen had been heading back to the shore with their night's catch. He says the time was just past nine. They had cooked their breakfast of rice and fish on the boat, dished it out and sat down to eat. The tsunami had crashed into the land as they sat watching the shore.

"We were about a mile away and could see the entire strip of coast from Hambantota to Kirinda. Suddenly we saw a wave rising as high as the sky and the land got completely covered. We didn't know what was happening. We stopped the boat and watched," Shihabi tells me. He and the other fishermen had seen the waves take back to the sea, people, parts of houses and trees. The water around their boat had not changed.

While Shihabi and the fishermen watched the waves hitting the land, Hanise, a fisher merchant, had been supervising the returning boats. Hanise lives down a narrow road

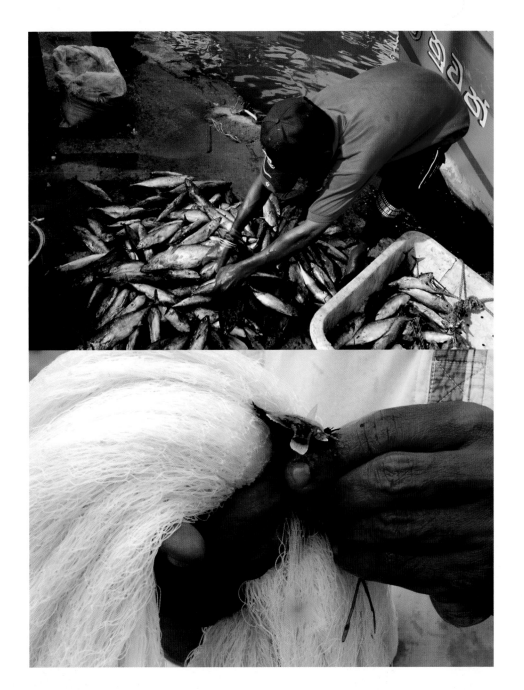

The fish that has been unloaded at the harbour are sorted into trays filled with blocks of ice in preparation for the journey out of Hambantota.

It takes nimble fingers to clean and repair a fishing-net without ripping it.

that leads to a small cove close to the harbour. This strip of beach is one of the places where the day's catch is unloaded. Hanise owns several boats and a small cold-room for storage annexed to his house. He says the sea had been very rough that morning. "Like a pan of milk," he says, "that was frothing on the fire."

Hanise had been watching the sea as it kept on rising. He says, "We are used to the sea rising like this so no one really took any notice. We just tied the boats. But this time the water did not stop rising. It kept on rising higher and higher. Then, before we knew it the water was completely in and people started running. I also ran. The water was at our heels. I got home and took my children and kept on running. We all managed to get to that hilly area in the town."

Hanise's wife had gone to the Hambantota Town market to buy the provisions for the week. His children, a daughter and a son of 15 and 12 years, had been at home. From the high ground at the top of the road, Hanise had watched the water come in to the beach that he had been on a few minutes ago. He had also watched the waves smother the market where he knew his wife was at the time. His wife did not survive. Hanise's eyes fill with tears, "We were married for 19 years," he says. "And she was 43."

Hanise and all the others had lost their boats. The storage room that Hanise had built had been completely destroyed. He points to the strip of wall between the main door of the house and the roof and says, "the water mark was there.' In early 2005 Hanise had remarried. He has moved back into the house.

Shihabi and the other fishermen had steered their way back to the shore by two in the afternoon. They had not been able to dock the boat and had stayed on it until late evening that day. The high water and the debris in the surrounding sea had prevented them from getting off. The people on the shore had been too distracted with the chaos to take time to draw the boat in. Shihabi's home is several kilometres in land and no one had been harmed.

Today, a morning at the harbour is no different from those before the tsunami. If you watch the cove from the Hambantota Rest House which has been built directly over it, you will see boats coming in with the night's catch. And over the breaking waves you will hear the sounds of men at work and water lapping the moored boats. The fishing industry in Hambantota is in motion. Nothing seems to have happened here.

The Sunday Market

THERE IS NO LONGER a Sunday market on the beach in the Hambantota Town. Before the tsunami, every Sunday morning villagers from as far inland as *Suriyaweva* would come with their fare to the market: old women with vegetables grown in their back gardens for extra income, and farmers with curd, eggs and agricultural produce from Hambantota. Many of the regular customers to the market came from far outside Hambantota Town.

Several years ago, the strip of beach that was used for the market, which lies behind an allotment of houses and shops, had been bare. The market had been moved to this strip of beach by the *Urban Council*, temporarily, with the intention of moving it back to a permanent venue once a suitable site had been selected. However, it had stayed on at the short-term venue to become a permanent feature in the lives of the residents of Hambantota: an administrative blunder for which the entire District was to pay a terrible price. The Hambantota Town market recorded the largest number of deaths in the tsunami in Sri Lanka within the ground area it covered. It is estimated that over 1000 people lost their lives.

The vehicle that I am in takes the dirt road that runs parallel to the beach. On either side, the land is barren except for a few wooden shacks. Cattle graze the ground that has only the occasional patch of faded grass. Here and there the ground is marked by cement foundations of buildings that had been washed away by the waves. It's a Sunday today, but the only people around are those who live in wooden makeshift houses.

The beach is a few feet below us and from the road we can only see a vast blue sky. On the 26th of December 2004 this strip of land took the worst of the waves with the water crashing inland as far as two kilometres. There were very few survivors.

We walk to one of the makeshift houses that has been built a few yards away from the beach. Planks have been put up on the square of cement that was once the floor of a house. Marlia Ahamed comes to the door to greet us. She calls me in and I sit down. She has partitioned the inside of her home with cloth to separate the small visitor's area from the sleeping area. Marlia raises the 'curtain' and shows me the 'room' which is the length and breadth of a bed. This space is crammed with clothes tied in large bundles and boxes stuffed with household items. They cook outdoors.

Marlia tells me how her family escaped, "That day my family was in different places. My husband and son had gone to get something and my daughter had gone for tuition lessons to Matara. Only my disabled mother and I were in the house. Suddenly I heard a terrible sound and then I was hit by the water. That is all I remember." She had been found, that afternoon about 2 kilometres inland, semi-conscious, under a towering pile of rubble. Rescuers had spent several hours removing the debris to release her and had been able to take her to hospital only in the evening. One of her legs had been badly hurt. In the days after the tsunami the doctors had thought that they may have to amputate the leg, but had later been able to spare it. She shows me her left thigh from which a chunk of flesh the size of a small apple has been removed. All that remains is a deep hole in the muscle.

Marlia's mother was not found. Her sisters and next of kin had lived in the neighbouring houses. None of them had survived: she had lost a total of eleven close relatives. Her survival

OVERLEAF

The Hambantota Town Market used to be more crowded than this market in another part of the district. It was on a narrow, short strip of land parallel to the beach.

89

is an exception. Most of the people who did survive the tsunami in this area around the market were those who had been away at the time. These include Marlia's husband and her two children. Mr. Raufdeen is another.

A New House

TODAY, MR. RAUFDEEN lives in a house he has received from a charity. The house is on a large acreage of land that has been allocated by the government for tsunami housing projects.

By the time we reach Mr. Raufdeen's house it is almost dusk. The door of the house is open, as in the case of all the houses around us, so we enter and wait. The sun shines on to the porch and light filters in to the house. It reveals a patina of dust on every surface of the house, the floor, the chairs and the raggedy wooden table at the far end. There is neither a new television nor expensive curtains in this house.

A general, undirected, cry goes from door to door for Mr. Raufdeen as neighbours and the stragglers around the estate inform him that he has visitors. A few minutes later Mr. Raufdeen walks in. When I see him and even before he talks to me I understand the dust and the emptiness of the house. His face is drawn, there is a vacant look in his eyes and he seems like a man who has never slept. This man has lost his spirit.

He sits down with a wry smile and starts talking about the events of the 26th of December. That morning, Mr. Raufdeen had been at a lathe workshop. "I started running home from the workshop when I heard about the waves. On my way I saw a woman on a *kohomba* tree and she called out to me to help her get down. I told her I couldn't stop. I kept on running, I saw a man on the ground bleeding, but I couldn't stop. I kept on running. When I got to the house everything was gone." His eyes fill with tears.

Mr. Raufdeen watches us
leave the housing estate.

He continues, "My wife, my son, my daughter, my sister-in-law and her child. And there was nothing of the house left. Nothing. Not even the bricks." Mr. Raufdeen's children had been eleven and thirteen years old. His wife had been forty two.

"It's the evenings that are the worst," he says. "Food is not a problem...I just go to my sister's house or a neighbour's and there is always something for me, but when I am here in the evenings I remember how we all used to sit down in the evenings and watch TV...."

He continues, "Those days when I fell ill I used to pray to God to make me better, but now I pray to God to let me die."

"I was married for 15 years," he says.

"And I married a bit late. People who have re-married and started all over again after the tsunami are saying that it is never the same. It's not the same you know," he tells me. Mr. Raufdeen has not considered re-marrying. He tells me that his neighbours are telling him it is time he re-married.

"I am 58 years now. It's hard to even start thinking about starting life all over again. But people are saying that I should. Maybe I should." He doesn't appear to speak with conviction.

Mr. Raufdeen is not the only one who has suffered loss. Most of his neighbours have also lost loved ones. Therefore there is a sense of looking out for each other. Some come by and help Mr. Raufdeen around the house, they repair the faulty electrical system and help with broken gutters. As we leave the house, children are gathering for the evening at his veranda. A couple of teenagers are sweeping the porch. Mr. Raufdeen's life is being nudged on by those around him.

A few weeks before this book went into print, six months following our meeting, I heard that Mr. Raufdeen had remarried.

The women listen to Buddhist monks chanting while they wait for the milk in the clay pot to boil over. The overflowing pot of milk symbolises that good fortune will come to the new building they have moved into after the tsunami.

Adopting Sri Lanka

THE WAVY OCEAN HOTEL in Tangalle is the perfect budget hideaway. The rooms are scrupulously clean: the walls washed in light colours and the beds covered with fresh linen. Downstairs, looking out to sea, is a dining room with a few tables and the kitchen next to it. At the edge of the hotel, the ground slopes to meet the beach.

The kitchen is the heart of the Wavy Ocean Hotel. Keerti Wedarachchi, who owns the Wavy Ocean Hotel, is cooking. He tosses a handful of large prawns into a pan on the fire. The prawns sizzle and settle down to a shimmer. Chunks of tomato, capsicum and fat rings of onion follow. He gives everything a liberal sprinkle of chilli powder and salt before pouring in vinegar and water. The room fills with the distinct smells of a favourite Sri Lankan dish: *devilled prawns*. The prawns will be accompanied by a bowl of steaming *yellow rice*, local rice cooked with turmeric for its colour and fragrant spices, a stick of cinnamon, a few pods of cardamoms, a spoonful of cloves and a leaf of pandunus torn from a tree in the garden.

I ask Keerti where he picked up his culinary skills. He laughs. Keerti had worked on cargo ships for many years and had travelled the world observing the cooks on ships at work and tried out new types of food at the ports they anchored. He had returned home to settle down when he had had "enough of the sea" and using all his savings, he had started the hotel.

Keerti had spent much of most of his life at sea and yet he says he will never comprehend the form the sea took as a tsunami. He tells me that everything he had was washed away by it, the business and his house which is on higher ground next to the hotel. Keerti points to the roof of his house, "That was the level of the water. We managed to swim over and climb our way out. My leg was hurt. But none of the guests was harmed."

Most of the small guest houses along the coast are back in business, revamped and modernised, through funding from donors.

"One foreigner who had come to this beach for a swim died. She was too close to the sea to get away. The waves came in so suddenly, you know." He says that she had drowned but her body had not been washed away.

"I brought the corpse in here. Her clothes had got ripped off. There was nothing I could do. I had only the sarong I was wearing so I covered the body with it."

I picture the place immediately after the waves had receded. The house and the hotel shattered: Keerti looking on at his life's work which has been ruined, contemplating where he would live and what he could salvage for his family. Yet, amidst all that, taking the time to cover a broken body and give it back its dignity. "Last year her family came to Sri Lanka," Keerti tells us, "and they performed a memorial for her at the spot she died."

The prawn curry is ready. He pours it into a ceramic dish, switches off the gas burner and guides us back into the dining room. A waiter brings us bottles of chilled ginger beer to the table.

"Come," he says, "sit down and enjoy the drinks. The sun is very hot today." After two years, the Wavy Ocean Hotel is back in business.

"Initially, the donors didn't focus on small hotels and guesthouses on the beach. The Government had brought in the 100 meter building reservation which stopped them getting involved in reconstruction along the coast right after the tsunami," says Geoffrey Dobbs[40], the founder of *The AdoptSriLanka Trust*[41]. Keerti's guesthouse, The *Wavy Ocean Hotel*, is one of the 125 hotels that would not have been back in business so soon unless it had been funded by *AdoptSriLanka* despite the red tape and the bureaucracy.

"I am an hotelier, so naturally I wanted to assist the small guesthouse owners," he adds with a glint in his eyes. *AdoptSriLanka* had received funds from the *Rough Guide Book series, The Mandarin Hotel, PATA* and the *Kadoori Foundation* to support small hotels.

Wavy Ocean Hotel
was helped to bounce back
by Adoptsrilanka with
funds provided by Rough Guides
ROUGH
GUIDES

Keerti Wedarachchi

"The hotel project was only just one area. We started right after the tsunami, with our own money, to help fishermen repair their boats. Then as we received contributions from donors we began twinning schools with schools overseas for assistance, built houses and even began a programme to teach people to swim. And then, there was also, Project *Fish and Ships*!"

Project *Fish and Ships* had been in response to the primary need for boat repairs and the secondary need to promote the consumption of fish as seafood sales plummeted when rumours spread that fish had been contaminated by human carcasses. *AdoptSriLanka* opened their own boat repair yard and by the end of the initial reconstruction phase had repaired several hundreds of boats. The programme to promote fish consumption had begun with a seafood festival in Mirissa, which moved on to an event at *Temple Trees*, the Prime Minister's Official residence, and had culminated with a motion being passed in the British Parliament to import more tuna from Sri Lanka.

The work of *AdoptSriLanka* has been remarkable for the reach it has made across the south of Sri Lanka and for the cross-section of people the organisation has been able to assist. The trust had segmented its work into project sectors such as *livelihoods regeneration, housing, trauma relief, conservation, pre-school building programmes* and several others. As *AdoptSriLanka* was set up exclusively for tsunami relief work by Geoffrey, it had been able to focus on meeting the reconstruction needs of the area. However, today, the trust no longer focuses entirely on tsunami reconstruction but has taken an active part in more programmatic work aimed at tackling broader issues in the region such as the need for revival of tourism, healthcare and education. It has, for instance, been involved in developing the second children's hospital in Sri Lanka. The approval of the trust's work from the coastal community has been unanimous. The success of an organisation such as *AdoptSriLanka* is essentially the ability to raise funds and utilise them with sensitivity to a community's needs and thereby gain credibility within the local social framework it is working in. This was possible because the founders were able to work at ground level while making use of their personal and professional contacts within the global community.

Geoffrey has been in Sri Lanka for over 10 years. He pioneered the concept of boutique hotels in Sri Lanka at a time when 'package tourism', characterised by piped music in lobbies and dining rooms overflowing with heavily laden buffet tables, was the only form of tourism that the travel traders in Sri Lanka felt safe to venture into. Today Geoffrey's boutique hotels are acknowledged by the local travel industry, if grudgingly, as the forerunners that carved out a successful market niche in Sri Lanka. When the tsunami took place and *AdoptSriLanka* was formed, Geoffrey's work in a glitzy global industry overlapped with the lives of coastal families. This overlapping of different worlds is a success because shrewd management of the market enabled the produce of coastal communities to become part of the lives of international consumers. In other words, the network of the global economy, self-serving capitalist forces and the power of savvy marketing had colluded for the larger good. There cannot be an image which captures *AdoptSriLanka's* success more powerfully than this – actress Christina Cole as Blanche Ingram, in the 2006 BBC production of *Jane Eyre*, wearing period costumes trimmed with handmade lace. The lace was produced in Sri Lanka by women who were assisted through *AdoptSriLanka's* livelihoods project.

New houses and build-
ings are replacing the
devastation caused
by the tsunami.

How Will We Remember?

I am talking about simply trying to tell them what it is like to stand where I do, and see the things I see. Sometimes these things fill me with horror, at other times they light up my senses.[42]

> Fergal Keane, *Letter to Daniel* (1996)

On the day of the tsunami the A2 highway was impassable. Today, on a quiet day, it is the perfect track for a man with a bike.

ON A QUIET SUNDAY afternoon, I sit outside Nihal's house with Dhammika, my unofficial guide for my days in Hambantota. The house is part of the stretch of commercial buildings that line either side of the A2 highway going into Hambantota Town. Most of the shops are closed today and the gravel paths that run along the road are empty of pedestrians. Our only distraction comes from the occasional vehicle that speeds past leaving us in a thin cloud of fumes and dust. Next to the house is a discarded fibreglass boat - a tsunami gift that has not been in use.

Nihal lives on the second floor of the house and the ground level has been converted into his business premises. Nihal is an undertaker. His wife Sumana has informed us that Nihal is away. Yet, Dhammika feels it is important for me to meet Nihal and his family as part of my travels around Hambantota as I collect snapshots of places, people and their lives two years after the tsunami. So we sit and wait. Dhammika explains to me why I should talk to Nihal and the others I have been meeting during my visit. There are places he feels I should

see: the marshland along the A2 which was strewn with bodies after the tsunami, but which is now once again a stretch of scrub. He tells me anecdotes of people's experiences: the incident of the army officers involved in clearing the dead bodies and the debris who lost their appetite and were not able eat any food. Dhammika tells me they lived on chocolate for days. He insists that I need to see these places and hear these people to understand where they were two years ago and how they have created their present.

Dhammika himself had not been directly affected by the tsunami as he lives away from the coast. Yet, no one in the District has been untouched because here, lives are interwoven by family ties, school friendships and professional affiliations. In one way or another, through the loss of a colleague, a friend or a relative, each person has felt the catastrophe. Each person has experienced and lived through the disaster personally.

I am meeting Dhammika and the people of the District two years after the tsunami devastated their world. Both of us know that what I am seeing does not capture the chaos during the first few months after the tragedy. Nor will any of the conversations with individuals who suffered losses capture the long journey each person has made through an inner landscape of hopelessness and pain to get to where they are two years on. Slowly and inevitably Hambantota has limped back to the everyday and the commonplace that hints of normalcy.

A few people of Hambantota such as Dhammika are attempting to reconcile the tsunami against the present and the future. They are aware that figures and statistics, the only objective evidence of the tragedy, convey little of the loss. On the other hand, there seems to be the realisation that memories are subjective and immensely personal; even those captured on film or paper. At the heels of this realisation is the unarticulated horror that time will dissipate the magnitude of the disaster when reconstruction is complete, painful memories heal and the present generation dies.

In less than two years, the disaster of the 26th of December 2004 has been overshadowed by the global events that succeeded it. Other catastrophes, natural disasters that caused upheaval and chaos, and wars - old and new – around the world have managed to attract the attention of the international public as well as Sri Lankans who live outside the areas affected by the tsunami. Public attention has shifted.   Then, how will the tsunami be remembered five years from now, a generation later?

As I travel around the District capturing images, memories and personal narratives, the only conclusion I come to is that this tragedy is too large and too horrific to be understood from one place and one time. People will be compelled to revisit the event many times, at different stages of their own lives and during different times in the history of the region to define the tragedy and what it means to them personally and collectively. Each definition and remembering may be no less truthful or accurate than the other. The lives and places that have been portrayed in this book too will continue to transform and change over the years. What has been captured here is what I saw and heard. I can only hope that I have transferred on to paper the essence of the memory that each person revealed to me at the time.

We never met Nihal that Sunday. His wife Sumana described to us how they coped with the endless stream of cortèges they had to arrange after the tsunami. We waited another half an hour for Nihal after our chat with her and left. To have stayed any longer would have meant overstepping Sumana's hospitality. She was pregnant with her second child and her household was getting ready for lunch.

A Legend

According to historical legend, recorded in the *Mahavamsa* and the *Rajavaliya*, the sea flooded the Kingdoms of Maya (in the West) and Ruhuna (in the South) in Sri Lanka during the reign of Kings Kelani Tissa and Kavan Tissa in the 2nd Century BC. [43]

King Kelani Tissa of Maya, on suspecting that a Buddhist monk was assisting the Queen and his brother in an adulterous relationship, ordered that the monk be killed in a vat of boiling oil. Soon after, the sea flooded the land, washing away 15 miles width of coastline[44]. The people, believing that the gods needed appeasement for the crime committed by the King, had requested him to make a sacrifice in atonement. The King sent his daughter, Devi, in a boat to sea as his offering to the Gods. The boat was swept ashore several days later in the South Western Coast of Sri Lanka where she was discovered by a group of fishermen. The King of Ruhuna, Kaavan Tissa, married the princess who was later known as Viharamahadevi.

According to R.L. Brohier, "At Gotimbaragodella, two miles inland from Kirinda, there stand the crumbling ruins of a *maligawa*, or palace, where Kavan Tissa is said to have officially welcomed and wed the princess; and finally, a medley of ancient of ancient monuments at Magul Maha Vihara – near Palatupana in the Ruhunu National Park – which mark the spot where the happy pair sojourned after their marriage."[45]

THE OLD VILLAGE HOUSE stands still in the August sun. Its white walls are thick as the legs of a fat elephant and cool as the water in the well at the end of the garden. The rains are late this year. The paddy is safe in the paddy chest and as dry as the crisp leaves that now float off the belli tree. Last year, the rains had come early and the paddy had been soaked in the field. Sometimes even the village doctor cannot tell if it will rain. There are times like that. This time, he had been right and the villagers were able to take their paddy in before the monsoon soaked the village and mixed the crisp leaves into the soft earth.

On the veranda sits an old woman. She is glad the uncooked rice she is holding on her lap is dry. And sitting there, as she searches for the unhusked grains that have crept into the rice, she sees the daughter of her fifth child on the steps of the veranda. She knows the child has nothing to do at this time of the day when people only sleep or wait in the veranda, here in this old house, away from her big city-school-friends and their toys.

So the old woman says, "Samudra." The child looks at her, so she continues, "Samudra, did you know that long long ago, in the times of our kings, on a day as hot as this, the sea came into our land?"

The child who is no more than eight, forgets this is an old woman telling a silly tale, and turns to her, eyes wide with disbelief.

"But why, why, archchi, how can that be?" says the child.

"Well," says old woman, "there was once a king."

"What was he like?" asks the child.

"Oh," says the old woman, "he was a powerful king."

"What else archchi," says the child, "didn't he have a palace?"

"Oh yes, yes, a large palace made of gold and he lived there with a beautiful queen. So beautiful that all the people in the country knew that she was a goddess that had come down to this land. But the king was jealous of other's love for her and he burnt his brother," says the woman.

"And a Buddhist sadhu. In a vat of hot oil."

The child remains silent.

"This made the gods who had sent the queen to this country angry because they knew she was good and that no matter how many people looked at her, she would still love the king."

"What did they do archchi?" the child asks.

The old woman says, "they sent the sea into the country."

"The sea!" the child exclaims.

"Yes, the sea came in and in and in and there was no longer any place for people to run. Their houses were taken away, their cats and dogs and children and trees got washed into the sea. The king knew he had to do something to say he was sorry to the gods."

"What did he do archchi, did he give all his gold?"

"Yes something as precious as gold. He gave them his daughter. He put her in a beautiful ship and sent her out to the sea, all alone, to say sorry to the Gods."

"Why didn't *he* go archchi," says the child with indignation.

"No, no my child, don't you know," says the old woman, "that only we women can talk to the Gods. So, the king made the Gods happy with the gift of his daughter, and slowly the water stopped coming in and because the princess was good and beautiful, the Gods did not kill her. They put her to sleep and slowly, gently, took the boat to the other end of the country."

"Oh I am so happy," says the child.

"Yes and do you know what happened to her?"

"No! archchi, no!"

"Well, when the fishermen on the beach saw that a beautiful princess had come to their shore, they ran to their king and told him about the princess. Their king came and took the beautiful princess to his palace and married her. And do you know the name of the king and this queen?" asks the old woman from her grandchild.

Before the child could answer, the child's parents drive into the garden. The leaves of the belli tree rustle as a flock of sleeping seven sisters flies in to the sky chattering angrily about the noise that awoke them.

The child runs to her parents shouting, "Do you know, do you know, that long time ago our land burnt and the sea came in and the king sent his daughter out to sea?"

The husband of the old woman's fifth child laughs and says, "Silly village tales, how can the sea come in? That will never happen."

Appendix

Countries affected by the 2004 Indian Ocean Tsunami

Country	Deaths		Injured	Missing	Displaced
	Confirmed	Estimated			
Indonesia	130,736	167,736	—	37,063	500,000
Sri Lanka	30,322	35,322	21,411		516,150
India	12,405	18,045	—	5,640	647,599
Thailand	53,953	8,212	8,457	2,817	7,000
Somalia	78	289	—	—	5,000
Myanmar	61	400	45	200	3,200
Maldives	82	108	—	26	15,000
Malaysia	68	75	299	6	—
Tanzania	10	13	—	—	—
Seychelles	3	3	57	—	200
Bangladesh	2	2	—	—	—
South Africa	24	2	—	—	—
Yemen	2	2	—	—	—
Kenya	1	1	2	—	—
Madagascar	—	—	—	—	1,000
Total	227,747	230,210	30,271	45,752	1,695,149

Impact of the Tsunami on Sri Lanka

Sri Lanka	Damaged Houses		Total Population	Affected Families	Total affected population	Displacement		Total dead, injured or missing
	Completely	Partially				Families	Individuals	
Northern Province								
Jaffna	6084	1114	589,000	14767	49270	10637	40117	4827
Killinochchi	1250	4250	140,000	N/A	51020	318	1603	1231
Mullativu	3400	600	141,000	6745	27057	6007	22557	6142
Vavuniya	N/A	N/A	138,250	N/A	3113	N/A	N/A	N/A
North Western Province								
Puttlam	23	72	722,000	N/A	850	18	66	8
Eastern Province								
Trincomalee	5974	10394	377,000	30547	86054	27746	83570	1415
Batticaloa	15939	5665	536,000	63717	186743	12494	62778	6167
Ampara	14403	6940	605,000	58616	183647	32385	123786	17677
Southern Province								
Hambantota	2303	1744	533,000	13493	27351	3334	17742	5824
Matara	2362	5659	780,000	19744	25445	2862	12019	8607
Galle	5970	6529	1,011,000	24853	58239	1472	127598	5085
Western Province								
Kalutara	2780	3116	1,077,000	9752	44411	6905	30193	811
Colombo	3398	2210	2,305,000	9647	19872	5290	31820	155
Gampaha	292	307	208,000	6827	32000	308	1449	14
Total	64178	48600	9,162,250	258708	795072	109776	555298	57963

This appendix was compiled by gathering data from various sources which include the Deptartment of Census and Statistics od Sri Lanka, reports by multilateral organisations and official country websites. The data varied from one source to another.

Impact of the Tsunami on Hambantota

Hambantota District	Impact on Properties						Impact on lives	
	Total area (ha)	Total area affected (ha)	Affected area as a % of total area	Number of GN Divisions affected	Damaged Houses		Affected families	Affected persons
					Completely	Partially		
DS Division								
Tangalle	825	153	5.4	28	920	710	6553	30965
Ambalantota	1137	248	4.6	8	179	335	2107	10035
Hambantota	2487	477	5.2	11	1059	630	5706	27522
Tissamaharamaa	1471	1057	1.4	3	145	69	1910	7648
Belliatte	–	–	–	–	–	–	194	756
Weerakatiya	–	–	–	–	–	–	154	606
Wallasmulla	–	–	–	–	–	–	35	140
Katuwana	–	–	–	–	–	–	48	187
Okewella	–	–	–	–	–	–	12	47
Angunukolapelessa	–	–	–	–	–	–	41	162
Sooriyawewa	–	–	–	–	–	–	118	462
Lunugamvehera	–	–	–	–	–	–	116	438
Total	5920	1935	3.1	50	2303	1744	16994	78968

Human Cost on Countries Outside the Tsunami Affected Region

The following countries reported dead or missing nationals as a result of the 2004 Indian Ocean tsunami

Argentina: 2 people dead
Australia: 26 people dead
Austria: 86 people dead
Belgium: 11 people dead
Brazil: 2 people dead
Canada: 15 people dead; 12 people injured; 5 people missing
Chile: 2 people dead
China: 3 people dead; 13 injured; 7 missing
Colombia: 1 person dead; 3 people injured
Croatia: 1 person dead
Czech Republic: 7 people dead; 5 injured
Denmark: 45 people dead; 1 person missing
Estonia: 3 people dead
Finland: 179 people dead
France: 95 people died; 189 people injured

Germany: 537 people dead; 15 people missing and presumed dead
Greece: 3 people missing; 1 person injured
Hong Kong: 38 people dead; 2 people missing
Ireland: 4 people dead
Israel: 6 people dead; 1 person missing
Italy: 40 people dead
Japan: 37 people dead; 7 people missing
Luxembourg: 2 people dead
Mexico: 2 people dead; 1 person missing
New Zealand: 6 people dead
Norway: 84 people dead
Philippines: 8 people dead
Poland: 1 person dead; 12 people missing

Portugal: 4 people dead; 4 people missing
Republic of China: 3 people dead
Russia: 2 people dead: 7 people missing
Singapore: 9 people dead
South Africa: 14 people dead
South Korea: 17 people dead; 3 people missing
Spain: 2 people dead
Sweden: 543 people dead
Switzerland: 106 people dead; 6 people missing
Turkey: 1 person dead
Ukraine: 2 people missing
United Kingdom: 149 people dead; 1 missing
United States: 18 people dead; 15 people missing, presumed dead
Vietnam: 1 person dead; 3 injured

Endnotes

[1] Woolf, Leonard. *Growing – an Autobiography of the Years 1904 – 1911*, The Hogarth Press, London, 1967, pp. 176 -177.

[2] Interviews in Hambantota, Tangalle and Colombo, September - November, 2006

[3] 'What does "tsunami" mean', *University of Washington*, university website: **geophys.washington.edu/tsunami/general/physics/meaning.html**, 20 November 2006

[4] 'What Cause Tsunamis?', *National Weather Service*, NWS website: **nws.noaa.gov/om/brochures/tsunami.htm**, 20 November 2006

[5] 'Long period seismic moment of the 2004 Sumatra earthquake and implications for the slip process and tsunami generation', *Northwestern University*, University website: **earth.northwestern.edu/people/seth/research/sumatra2.html**, 20 November 2006

[6] 'The December 26, 2004 Indian Ocean Tsunami: Initial Findings on Tsunami Sand Deposits, Damage, and Inundation in Sri Lanka', *U.S. Geological Survey*, 2005. USGS website: **walrus.wr.usgs.gov/tsunami/srilanka05/**. 20 November 2006

[7] Ibid.

[8] Unless specified otherwise, *Hambantota* refers to the Hambantota District throughout this book

[9] 'A Report on ADB's Response to the Asian Tsunami,' *Asian Development Bank*, 2005. ADB website: **adb.org/Documents/Reports/ADB-Tsunami/tsunami-highlights.pdf**, March 2007

[10] Brohier, R.L. *Seeing Ceylon*, Lake House Investments, 1971, p. 199.

[11] 'Sampan', *The American Heritage® Dictionary of the English Language, Fourth Edition*, Answers.com, 03 Nov. 2006

[12] Dewaraja, Lorna. *Muslims of Sri Lanka – One Thousand Years of Ethnic Harmony*, The Sri Lanka Islamic Foundation, Colombo, 1994. p. 46

[13] 'Tsunami Tragedy: in Numbers'. *LMD –The Voice of Business*, April. 2005, pp. 108- 109

[14] Interview with Franz Meyer, November 2006, Colombo

[15] 'Post Tsunami Recovery and Reconstruction.' *Joint Report by the Government of Sri Lanka and Development Partners*, December 2005, p. vii

[16] Interview with Franz Meyer, November 2006, Colombo

[17] Source: project website - **tangallehospital.com/Project_status.html**

[18] 'Tsunami Aid Retrospective.' *Der Spiegel*, 2005, website: **spiegel.de/international/0,1518,392411,00.html**, Dec, 2006

[19] 'Tsunami Aid Retrospective.' *Der Spiegel*, 2005, website: **spiegel.de/international/0,1518,392411,00.html**, Dec, 2006

[20] Source: **manchester-enterprises.com**, 2007

[21] *The Island*, Vol. 26 . No. 276, Late City Edition, 16th Nov. 2006.

[22] Ryan, Carolyn. *"Tsunami Boost for Mental Health Care"*, BBC News, BBC News website, 22 December 2005. **news.bbc.co.uk/1/hi/health/4524804.stm**, November 2006.

[23] Ibid

[24] Ibid

[25] 'Sri Lanka: Mental Health and Policy Service Development Projects'. *World Health Organisation*, WHO website: **who.int/mental_health/policy/en/Sri%20Lanka.pdf**, Dec, 2006

[26] Interviews in Hambantota, September 2006.

[27] Kübler-Ross MD, Elizabeth. *On Death and Dying*, Routledge, London and New York, 1995, p 44

[28] Cutler, Howard & Dalai Lama. *The Art of Happiness.* Coronet Books, London, 1999, pp.120 - 121

[29] Source: **adb.org/Documents/Reports/Tsunami/sri-lanka-annex13.pdf**

[30] Ibid

[31] Creech, Steve. Lecture delivered at the US-SL Fulbright Commission, October, 2005

[32] Hussain, Asgar. Is it Safe to Eat Fish? *LMD –The Voice of Business*, April. 2005, pp 167-168

[33] Source: **youth-business.org**, 2007.

[34] Interview with Mr. B.L. Ramanayake, Colombo, 2007

[35] Interview with Rainer Frauenfeld, Country Director - UNOPS, in Colombo, 2007

[36] Woolf, Leonard. *The Village in the Jungle*, Oxford University Press, Chennai, 2000, pp 4-5

[37] Smith, Michael York. *Hambantota District – Sri Lanka – A Description* , Royal Norwegian Ministry of Development Cooperation, Colombo, 1986.

[38] Source: **tafren.wow.lk/detail_dis.php**, 2006

[39] The family profiled in this chapter wished to remain anonymous. All names of individuals and places have been changed.

[40] Interview with Geoffrey Dobbs in Colombo, 2007

[41] Source: **adoptsrilanka.com**, 2007

[42] Keane, Fergal. *Letter to Daniel – Despatches from the Heart,* Penguin Books, London, 1996, p. 10

[43] Hewapathirana, Daya. 'History of Tsunamis in Sri Lanka', *Sunday Observer,* 21. 2. 2005, Online Edition: **sundayobserver. lk/2005/01/02/fea29.html**; December 2006.

[44] Brohier, R.L. *Seeing Ceylon*, Lake House Investments, 1971, p. 203

[45] Ibid.

Bibliography

Brohier, R.L. *Seeing Ceylon*, Lake House Investments, 1971

Cutler, Howard & Lama, Dalai. *The Art of Happiness.* Coronet Books, London, 1999

Dewaraja, Lorna. *Muslims of Sri Lanka – One Thousand Years of Ethnic Harmony*, The Sri Lanka Islamic Foundation, Colombo, 1994

Keane, Fergal. *Letter to Daniel – Despatches from the Heart,* Penguin Books, London, 1996

Kübler-Ross MD, Elizabeth. *On Death and Dying*, Routledge, London and New York, 1995

LMD –The Voice of Business, April, 2005

Smith, Michael York. *Hambantota District – Sri Lanka – A Description*, Royal Norwegian Ministry of Development Cooperation, Colombo, 1986

Woolf, Leonard. *Growing – an Autobiography of the Years 1904 – 1911*, The Hogarth Press, London, 1967

Woolf, Leonard. *The Village in the Jungle*, Oxford University Press, Chennai, 2000

Joint Report by the Government of Sri Lanka and Development Partners, December, 2005

Index

Designed and typeset by Deshan Tennekoon
Printed and bound in Sri Lanka by Gunaratne Offset Ltd.

Typeset in Georgia 10/16
Printed on 120GSM Matt Art Paper